HITLER

IN THE CROSSHAIRS

Also by John Woodbridge

Revolt in Prerevolutionary France

Letters along the Way (with D. A. Carson)

A God-Sized Vision (with Colin Hansen)

The Mark of Jesus (with Timothy George)

Biblical Authority

Also by Maurice Possley

Everybody Pays: Two Men, One Murder and the Price of Truth
(Maurice Possley and Rick Kogan)

The Brown's Chicken Massacre

A GI'S STORY OF COURAGE AND FAITH

HITLER
IN THE CROSSHAIRS

JOHN WOODBRIDGE
& MAURICE POSSLEY
Pulitzer Prize-Winning Journalist

ZONDERVAN®

ZONDERVAN.com/
AUTHORTRACKER
follow your favorite authors

ZONDERVAN

Hitler in the Crosshairs
Copyright © 2011 by Maurice Possley and John Woodbridge

This title is also available as a Zondervan ebook.
Visit www.zondervan.com/ebooks.

This title is also available in a Zondervan audio edition.
Visit www.zondervan.fm.

Requests for information should be addressed to:

Zondervan, *Grand Rapids, Michigan 49530*

ISBN 978-0-310-32587-1

Published in association with Yates & Yates, www.yates2.com.

Cover design: Jason Gabbert / Faceout Studio
Cover image: Shutterstock®
Interior design: Beth Shagene
Map design: Ruth Pettis
Editing: Sue Brower and Bob Hudson

Printed in the United States of America

11 12 13 14 15 16 /DCI/ 24 23 22 21 20 19 18 17 16 15 14 13 12 11 10 9 8 7 6 5 4 3 2 1

*For those men and women
who served and continue to serve
both God and country in the Armed Forces.*

*For W. J. Frerichs, who served in harm's way
in the South Pacific during World War II
and returned home.*

*For Harold J. Possley, and his two brothers,
Leroy H. Possley and Frances R. Possley,
all of whom served during
World War II and returned home.*

*And in memory of their brother,
Maurice M. Possley,
a ball turret gunner on a B-24
killed in action
in the Pacific on September 1, 1944.*

The foxhole rifleman, the epitome of the fighting soldier, comprises only a few percent of the total forces. But he has endured the heat and cold, and mud and dust, and the almost intolerable fatigue and strain. His flesh, his spirit, and his nerve have had to accept and withstand hardships and dangers which literally defy description.

He bore the great burden of the casualty cost and he makes up the great part of the population of the silent cemeteries overseas. Where he was, there the battle was. He took the ground and held it. Most of the sweat and blood were his; his family shed most of the tears.

We should never forget that our finest weapons are only as good as the heart of the man that uses them.

June 26, 1954, General Charles L. Bolte,
Vice Chief of Staff, U.S. Army

AUTHORS' NOTE

The events depicted in this book are based on a multitude of sources and are true to the best of our belief and knowledge. In some instances, narrative scenes and dialogue have been recreated based on interviews, letters, and other archival documents and presented in a manner that we believe is faithful to the individuals and the events portrayed.

John Woodbridge and Maurice Possley

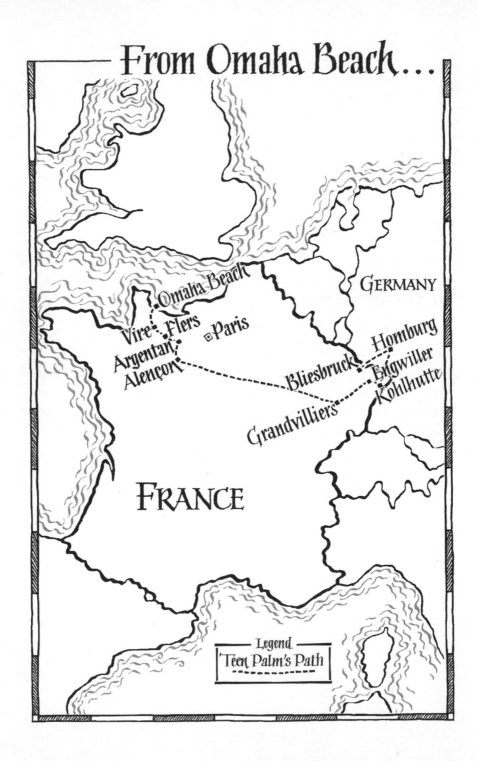

HITLER

IN THE CROSSHAIRS

PROLOGUE

THE PAST IS ALWAYS WITH US, EVEN AS IT STEADILY SLIPS away, becoming ever more silent in the shadows of our lives. And so it was on the night of December 22, 2005, as snow drifted down gently in the darkness, softening the edges of the handsome homes and glistening the broad yards on the outskirts of Lake Forest, a suburb north of Chicago. John Woodbridge, a history professor at nearby Trinity International University, walked into the family room of his house, turned on the television set, and sat down on the couch to watch the evening news. This is what he did most nights, without consequence.

On the screen, beneath the image of a newsreader, words scrolled and Woodbridge was immediately riveted. This news ticker informed him that a gun believed to have once belonged to Adolf Hitler was being put up for auction by the owner of the Midwest Exchange pawnshop in downstate Bloomington. The gun was a model of craftsmanship, two 16-gauge shotgun barrels topped by a single 8mm rifle barrel and, most significantly, a stock that bore the initials "AH." It was said to have been taken from Hitler's secluded retreat in the Bavarian Mountains, about a hundred miles southeast of Munich, when it had been overrun by U.S. Army soldiers in the final bloody and chaotic days of World War II.

As Woodbridge read the words scrolling across the screen, he was grabbed by a misty memory, and in his mind he saw himself as a six-year-old in his home in Savannah, Georgia. He could hear the voice of his father say, "Come into my study," and there he watched as his father opened a drawer of his desk and withdrew from it a golden pistol.

"This gun belonged to Adolf Hitler," said his father, Charles.

The voices on the television faded as he concentrated, trying to add more detail to his memories. But the veil of time was nearly sixty years thick and he could recall nothing more.

He went into the kitchen where he found his wife, Susan, and told her what he was remembering.

"How in the world did my father get that pistol?" he asked. "How did such a thing wind up in the home of a Presbyterian minister?"

Susan opened her mouth to reply ...

"Wait, wait a second," Woodbridge said excitedly. "Teen Palm! I remember a man named Teen Palm. I think he was the one who gave it to my dad. Teen was a soldier in the war. A very good friend of my father's. Teen Palm."

Woodbridge paused and then said, "I wonder what happened to him."

Susan looked at him quizzically.

"We met his daughter, remember?" she said. "And we met Teen Palm's widow."

"We did?" Woodbridge said. "When was that?"

She reminded him of a mid-1980s trip to Camp of the Woods in Speculator, New York. This was the place where John and his three sisters had pleasantly spent summer vacations as children. On a return trip many years later, John and

Susan had been introduced to two other visitors, Teen Palm's widow, Helen, and their daughter, Susie.

Flabbergasted, Woodbridge said, "I don't recall that at all. What was Susie's last name?"

After searching through drawers in a kitchen cabinet, Susan triumphantly held up an old personal telephone directory. "Here's her number."

He dialed. Susie picked up on the second ring and, after a bit of introductory small talk, she said, "Of course I remember you. Your father was a very dear friend of my dad. Your father was the person who led my dad to faith in Christ."

"Did your father ever talk about his military career?" Woodbridge asked. "Did he ever talk about a gun, a gun that belonged to Adolf Hitler? Could he have given that gun to my father? Why would he give that gun to my father?"

It was now Susie's turn to be puzzled.

"No, he never mentioned it. He was in the Army but ... wait. I do have an old suitcase and several containers of my father's military records," she said. "And there are letters he wrote to my mother during the war, a lot of them. I have those."

She explained that her mother had become increasingly frail over the years and had ultimately come to live with Susie and her husband in New Jersey. When she arrived, she brought the suitcase and a burlap sack of memorabilia, including a German officer's helmet and a large Nazi flag.

Susie told Woodbridge she would go through the letters to see if she could find any correspondence between Teen Palm and Woodbridge's father, any mention of a gun.

Over the next few days, anxious for information, Woodbridge contacted his three sisters.

One by one, they answered:

They had seen the gun.

It came from a soldier named Teen Palm.

It was Adolf Hitler's pistol.

Woodbridge was energized, the historian in him hooked. The past had come roaring into his life, and he would not be satisfied until he was able to unravel the story of Teen Palm and, he thought with a shudder, Adolph Hitler's gun.

CHAPTER 1

"*IRA HENRY PALM.*"

The name echoed through the auditorium at Mount Vernon High School, and a young man rose from his chair in the third row and strode toward the stage wearing the wide, toothy grin that had long disarmed and charmed family and friends in this New York town less than twenty miles north of Manhattan.

Ever the athlete, he moved fluidly and confidently on this June evening in 1932. Still, he fought a ripple of unease. He knew that his academic record over the past four years was spotty at best, and he was not prepared to fully relax until Principal Hugh Stewart placed his diploma in his hand. For reasons that would ever remain a mystery, Palm's diploma bore the middle name of his older brother, Clifton, and not his true middle name, Arterburn. But over the years, he had made clear that he was not all that fond of the name Arterburn in the first place.

Arterburn was his mother's maiden name and came from a long line of pioneers who settled originally in the Shenandoah Valley of Virginia. Some of their descendants had loaded their possessions onto a flatboat and floated down the Ohio River until reaching the banks of Beargrass Creek in Louisville.

There the Arterburn family settled in St. Matthews, Kentucky, in the late eighteenth century. Over the next decades, the Arterburns established successful careers and excellent reputations as farmers, horsemen, bankers, and civic leaders. They attended colleges, including Yale. At one time, the family estate consisted of more than one thousand acres and by the mid-1850s, the Arterburns were living a life of comfort and ease, aided by resident slave families who took care of the household chores, attended to the needs of the children, cooked, raised crops, and managed the livestock.

Slavery was a big business in Kentucky at that time, and Louisville was the launching point for thousands of men and women to be shipped to large plantations farther south. While awaiting buyers, slaves were shackled together in pens at the four large slave markets operating there, including one owned by the Arterburns.

Mary Jane Taylor, a slave who helped care for the Arterburn children at this time, would say many decades later that life on the Arterburn estate was free from the cruelty and abuse frequently inflicted on slaves on farms and plantations across the South. After the Civil War, estate owner Norbourne Arterburn gave Christmas gifts and cash to all of the family's slaves and, she recalled, "Then he told us we were free."

It is impossible to know how heavily the stigma of slave trading hung over the family, but by the time Palm received his diploma, it had been erased from the name Arterburn. His mother, Susan, had been born in 1889, third of the eight children of Clifton C. and Georgia Arterburn, all of them living in a stately, two-story home surrounded by six hundred crab apple trees just outside Louisville.

Clifton, or C.C. as he was commonly known, was a horse breeder and sportsman who regularly traveled to Indiana and other states to race trotters. Sadly, his other passionate pursuits were heavy drinking and gambling, and as the twentieth century neared, the family reaped the sorrows of his bad habits: the farm and virtually every stick of furniture in the house had to be sold to pay off debts.

When a friend offered him a railroad job, the family moved to Mount Vernon, then a burgeoning town of twenty-one thousand whose growth was fueled by New York City residents fleeing the rising cost of living. The family had barely established a toehold there when, in brutal back-to-back fashion, Susan lost both of her parents. She was fifteen when her mother died after a short illness in 1905; the following year she lost her father when, drunk, C.C. toppled from a train platform and died under the wheels of a passing locomotive.

In 1907, eighteen-year-old Susan met twenty-six-year-old Fred Palm at a dance sponsored by the Mount Vernon Fire Department. A native of New York City, Fred was one of eight children and worked as a Mount Vernon firefighter, as did his father and one of his brothers. He and Susan married in November of that year, and though Susan was a Presbyterian, she consented to be married by a Catholic priest because Fred had been raised a Roman Catholic.

Their first child, Gladys, was born in 1909. The second, Clifton, arrived two years later, and Ira was born January 11, 1913. He weighed barely six pounds at birth, and family members and other relatives so frequently remarked on how "teeny" he was that he was dubbed "Teen," a nickname that stayed with him his whole life. The family's last child, Doris, was born in 1927.

They lived in a three-story frame home that was alive with activity during Teen's early years. Rooms on the top floor were rented out to college students, as well as to young men trying to launch their careers and the occasional relative who had fallen on hard times. These tenants, known collectively as "the boys," frequently joined the family for dinners and participated in animated discussions and played cards in the living room.

During the holidays, the dining room table groaned under the weight of plates and cutlery and food for as many as twenty family members, tenants, and friends. Afterward, as the adults conversed about politics, sports, and other news of the day, Teen would slip away either to play with the other children or find some sort of mischief.

The front door of the home opened onto an entrance hall and a staircase with a wooden banister. The only telephone in the house stood sentinel-like on a table. There were two connected living rooms, one dominated by a piano, where the family often gathered to sing whenever Gladys played. The rear living room, with its fireplace, was Fred's cozy retreat. He could often be found there, sitting in a large easy chair, munching jelly beans while listening to New York Yankees baseball games on his brown wooden RCA radio. Teen knew that if he really needed to speak with his father on a summer afternoon, he could find him in this room listening to the radio. In these days before air-conditioning, Fred Palm did not mind if the room got stuffy, and it did, as long as the Yankees won, and they did, dominated by Babe Ruth and Lou Gehrig from the time Teen was twelve.

Fred Palm was a quiet man who usually kept to himself, preferring solitude to the often-hectic household and the strains of family life. After being struck in the eye by a nail and therefore no longer able to work as a firefighter, he began to earn a modest living as a handyman and carpenter. But "Pop," as everyone called him, preferred to stay at home and seldom ventured out even when Susan and the children went on vacation or visited relatives. He was a tinkerer as well, and he shared his skills with his sons. By their mid-teens, Teen and Cliff were regularly and proficiently working on the family car and doing carpentry work.

Susan spent most of her time in the large and sunny kitchen at the back of the house. Teen adored his mother and was often in the kitchen, seeking her counsel or just to pass time as she kneaded dough, chopped onions, peeled apples for pie, or carried steaming platters of food into the adjoining dining room. Just before each meal was served, she would dash upstairs and change into a proper dress and jewelry before taking her place at the table. She was a lady, retaining many of the qualities of a southern belle

Soft-spoken and bubbling with charm, Susan was the epitome of poise. With her soft brown eyes and palpable calm, she was adept at defusing the tensest squabbles, solving the prickliest problems.

She ran the home and took care of the boarders. An excellent seamstress, she sewed clothes for the family to save money. Teen was fond of telling his childhood friends that if he ever had a million dollars, he would give her a box of Wheaties and a pile of diamonds.

Susan took Teen and Gladys to Sunday school at the nearby Presbyterian church. Susan had a beautiful singing voice and taught Teen to sing, chiding him to practice regularly, not at all reluctant to tell him when he was off key or when his timing was imprecise. At the urging of his mother, who somehow had managed to scrape up the money, Teen took saxophone lessons. He loved the instrument and became proficient so quickly that after his freshman year in high school, he and some friends formed a band that played regularly during summers at local clubs.

After his high school graduation ceremony, with his diploma firmly clenched in his hand, Teen partied with his friends. He was among the most popular students in the school. Handsome and outgoing, with what many said were "Hollywood good looks," Teen was also a talented athlete, good enough to have been offered a football scholarship to attend North Carolina State College of Agriculture and Engineering, in Raleigh, North Carolina.

One summer evening, not long after graduation, Teen paid a visit to the Savoy Ice Cream parlor, where, as a freshman four years earlier, he had worked as a soda jerk. He liked serving up tasty chocolate sodas, banana splits, and sundaes to customers sitting on parlor stools and facing him directly across the shiny metallic counter. The job had not lasted long. His fondness for ice cream was his undoing and he had been sneaking too many free samples.

On this night, as he sat in a booth, a few of the employees greeted him cordially and commented about his athletic scholarship. He was destined for stardom, they said. They echoed local sportswriters who had tagged him as one of the best high school players on the East Coast. One expressed the confidence that he would soon be reading of Teen's football exploits in the major New York City newspapers. Indeed, a number of sportswriters at those papers tabbed him as the equivalent of "All State." One friend said that he would eclipse the fame of another Mount Vernon native, Frank Carideo, who had gone on to be a star quarterback under Knute Rockne at the University of Notre Dame a few years earlier.

Politely, he acknowledged the praise, and soon he was alone with his thoughts, barely paying attention to his chocolate soda while staring out the window. It was hard for him to believe that his football days in Mount Vernon were over. How had they passed so quickly? He found himself feeling vaguely unsettled. The predictions of his friends felt less like encouragement than burden. Despite his athletic success, musical talent, and good looks, Teen battled a lack of self-confidence, nagged by the thought that he might be a flop as a football player in college and compounded by fears about his weak academic skills. Would he be swallowed in the shadow of his brother who was already at North Carolina State College of Agriculture and Engineering? Might it be better for him to stay in Mount Vernon, get a job, and live with his family?

A manifestation of Teen's self-doubts could be found in his selection of the motto that was placed adjacent to his senior yearbook photograph. It was awkward and enigmatic: "He wants to be good, but his eyes won't let him."

He also worried about the separation from his family — not just his parents, but particularly his mother's older sister, Nan. A second mother to him, Aunt Nan still called him "Little Boy," a habit that began when he fell ill as a youngster and she spent many hours at his bedside. Nan's only daughter, Marion, Teen's older cousin, had been lured into show business years earlier, and Nan frequently urged Teen to do the same, lauding his abilities as a singer and sax player. This wasn't empty talk. Aunt Nan knew show business. By the time Teen graduated from high school, Marion was singing and dancing in vaudeville. Marion's husband, Frank Martine, was an accomplished saxophonist and clarinetist who played in stage shows in the 1920s and would later perform with the Big Bands led by Paul Whiteman, Fred Waring, and the Dorsey bothers.

Over the years, Aunt Nan regaled Teen with stories. Marion

and her husband and their two children had lived next door to Bill "Bojangles" Robinson, the great American tap dancer, and occasionally dined with the star and his family. Marion had even performed on stage with Robinson. Nan told Teen that when Marion and her husband had lived on Long Island, they lived next door to Louis Prima, the famous jazz-man, singer, trumpeter, and actor. They were so close that Prima's mother babysat the couple's two boys. Marion herself often spoke of heading to Hollywood to become a movie star.

Performers peppered the family. Teen's older sister, Gladys, worked as a legal secretary during the day and at night was a tap dancer at Proctor's Theatre in Mount Vernon, well known for its vaudeville shows and the place where Babe Ruth had made his "singing" debut in 1921.

Teen was never much of a student, never at ease in the classroom. His home was the stage — singing and playing sax. He was more than pleased that his band had a number of appearances booked in the days before he was to leave for college. But he also wondered seriously if he should forget about college and instead try to get work with local bands around Mount Vernon and, perhaps, eventually hook up with a touring Big Band. Maybe Marion's husband could introduce him to some of his musician friends, the leaders of the bands that played at the Glen Island Casino, a popular dance club overlooking Long Island Sound.

Leaving the ice cream parlor for the short walk home, Teen was dreaming of his name in the headlines and on theater marquees while also hearing the words of Principal Stewart on graduation night when he admonished the senior class: "I would that your talents and those of the thousands of graduates of other schools might be dedicated to the perplexing problems of the day in such a manner that this year 1932 might mark the birth of a new era in the social, political, economic, and international history of our nation."

A week later, Teen was on stage singing and playing his saxophone with his band in a small New Rochelle club. Shortly after midnight, he and his friend Charles Tividy began the ten minute drive to Mount Vernon. As the car sped down Winyah Avenue, Tividy behind the wheel, the screeching of tires shattered the early morning stillness. That was followed by a booming crash as the car collided head-on with another vehicle. Tividy's sedan was pancaked over the other vehicle, and the front ends of both cars met in a terrifying mess of mangled bumpers, contorted wheels, and shattered headlights.

The impact propelled Teen through the front of the car and over the hood. Fortunately, there was no glass in the windshield. He lay on the ground, bleeding but conscious, as both cars burst into flames. People streamed from their homes and some pulled Teen, Tividy, and the driver of the other car away from the burning wreckage. A passing car was hailed to take them to the nearest hospital. Gingerly, Teen was placed in the back seat of the car, and off it sped. Fighting shortness of breath and wracked with pain, Teen could only nod when the driver said he would get him medical help as quickly as possible.

But incredibly, as the car sped away, it collided with another vehicle. Already experiencing pain in his chest after the first crash, Teen felt new pains attack the rest of his body. Minutes passed before he was extricated and transported in a third car to the hospital.

He was rushed into surgery and emerged several hours later in a body cast. His doctor told him, "You are lucky to be alive," and Teen understood and felt happy to be alive, and to learn that Tividy and the other driver had also survived. But he was staggered to hear he would be confined to bed for six months.

The implications were obvious. He was not going to attend college in the fall. He would not be playing football. There would be no scholarship. Would he ever be able to sing or play music again?

Slowly and painstakingly, drawing upon the determination that would later define his life, Teen fought his way back. When he was finally able to get free of the body cast, he was physically weak. But he was able to focus on and find great solace and hope in his music, practicing his saxophone and his repertoire of songs. And a year after the accident, he was once again going out regularly to dance and listen to music.

But despite his successful recovery, he felt adrift, his future uncertain. Money was tight at home. His father was finding fewer and fewer carpentry jobs. Teen considered seeking a full-time job so he could contribute to the economic support of his family. But what job?

Then, one hot summer day in 1933, the phone rang at the Palm household. The caller identified himself as Jimmy Poyner. He said he had met Cliff, Teen's older brother, while both were attending North Carolina State College. Poyner said he was putting together a band with other students from that college, Duke University, and the University of North Carolina.

"And we're calling ourselves the 'Southern Pines Orchestra,'" Poyner said.

He asked about Teen's car crash and his recovery, then got to the point: "Cliff says you've spent a lot of time at the Glen Island Casino. He tells me you listen a lot to the sweet music of Glen Gray and the Casa Loma Orchestra. He says you admire their singer, Kenny Sargent. Well, that's all well and good, but Cliff says you can sing just as good as Sargent."

Teen was stunned. Sargent was his idea of the perfect ballad singer.

"Thanks, Mr. Poyner," he said, shyly. "He is my favorite singer, all right. Really smooth."

"Right, I know," Poyner said. "But the rest of the boys and I want to invite you to try out for a position in our orchestra. Saxophonist and ballad singer. Why don't you come down to Raleigh a couple of days before school starts? A couple of the boys and I will meet you at the Raleigh train station. Then we'll head down to Southern Pines, where we've been practicing. You try out. If you're anything close to the musician your brother says you are, we want you in our band."

Poyner paused, awaiting a response. But Teen was too stunned to speak.

"Okay, then. Just think about it," Poyner said. "Don't decide now. But I hope I see you soon."

Dazed, Teen hung up the phone. As he tried to process what he had just heard, his mind was a wild swirl of questions: Could this be his big show business break? *What if he failed?* Could he make enough money as a musician to pay for his education now that his football scholarship was gone? *What if he failed?* Would his mother and father believe him a fool for trying to go to school and play in a band at the same time? *What if he failed? What if he failed? What if he failed?*

These thoughts, these worries, these questions dogged him for days and were still with him a week later when he walked into the Glen Island Casino. The dance floor, which could accommodate up to one thousand eight hundred people, was packed. Built in 1930, the casino had become one of the premier entertainment centers on the East Coast, with performances broadcast on radio to increasingly large audiences. Many of the great entertainers of the day performed here: the Dorsey brothers, Benny Goodman, Ozzie Nelson and his band, and on this night Glen Gray and the Casa Loma Orchestra, featuring the golden-throated Sargent.

As couples glided across the dance floor, others dined on white-linen-topped tables. With the last notes of "Doing the New York," the lights around the large dance floor dimmed. Sargent took his place underneath a spotlight and behind a microphone on the white riser bordering the dance floor. A minor stampede of dancers, including Teen, rushed toward the stage.

Sargent, dark-haired and handsome, ended the band's set with "Under a Blanket of Blue," and as the crowd broke into wild applause, Teen stepped off the dance floor and moved toward the open doors at the edge of the hall. He walked outside and looked up to see that thick clouds had rolled in, partially covering the moon. The breeze had strengthened, bringing a chill to the air. He could smell the sea and hear the lapping of waves on the beach below. He sat down on a plain park bench. Enveloped by the darkness and the quiet, he took a deep breath, and made his decision.

CHAPTER 2

THE REICHSTAG BUILDING IN BERLIN, HOME OF THE GERMAN Parliament, was on fire. A tremendous explosion had ripped into the great plenary hall of the building, and pillars of flame now shot through the roof as thick smoke billowed from open windows.

It was February 27, 1933, and a few blocks away, Adolf Hitler, Germany's new chancellor and the head of the Nazi Party, was attending a small dinner party at the home of Dr. Paul Joseph Goebbels, a close friend and Nazi supporter. A telephone call interrupted the meal.

Goebbels picked up the phone and heard the news. He and Hitler, without good-byes, immediately left the party, climbed into a car, and sped toward the Reichstag. A block away, they could see the building's ornate dome illuminated by the inferno.

The speed of the flames left no doubt in their minds: the fire had been deliberately set, and the likely culprits were Communists.

Already at the scene were Hermann Goering, another prominent Nazi, and Rudolf Diels, the head of the Gestapo, the official secret police of Nazi Germany. Goering was screaming at Diels: "This is the beginning of the Communist revolution!

We must not wait a minute. We will show no mercy. Every Communist official must be shot where he is found. Every Communist deputy must this very night be strung up."

The efficient Diels sent out the orders. Within an hour, prominent Communist politicians and journalists answered the knocks on their doors and were taken into custody.

Among the first arrested was Marinus van der Lubbe, a twenty-four-year-old Dutch Communist, seized and put in handcuffs as he stood outside the burning building. When authorities said he had confessed to setting the blaze, it gave solid credence to the Nazi claim that Communists were a grave threat to Germany. Months later, Lubbe was convicted and guillotined. By then it was evident that the torching of the Reichstag had initiated a bloody civil war and was fueling the rise of Adolf Hitler.

Born on April 20, 1889, in Braunau am Inn, Austria, Hitler was the son of Alois Hitler Schicklgruber, an Austrian customs agent and loyal defender of the Austro-Hungarian monarchy. He was a harsh disciplinarian and administered almost daily thrashings to his son.

In contrast, Klara Hitler, Hitler's mother and Alois's third wife, was a pious and kindly woman. Twenty years younger than Alois, she doted on Adolf and his younger sister, Paula, as well as the two children from her husband's second marriage, Alois and Angela.

Adolf, ever in fear of his father's outbursts, loathed him. But he deeply loved his mother; he carried her picture with him until his death. In 1898, the family moved to a village near Linz which Hitler would forever after claim as his home town.

He despised school and his teachers, except for one: Dr. Leonard Pötsch, a history teacher who sparked Hitler's imagination with stories of German heroism and the man credited with nurturing Hitler's hatred of Jews. By his mid-teens, Hitler was constantly clashing with his father over his career ambitions. Hitler wanted to become an artist. His father insisted he become a civil servant.

Their struggle ended on January 3, 1903, when Hitler's father died. Later that year, Hitler dropped out of school and for the next three years spent most of his time taking piano lessons, drawing, reading, and immersing himself in opera, enraptured by the emotionally charged music of Richard Wagner.

Hitler was greatly moved by Wagner's opera *Rienzi*. After Hitler saw it, his friend August Kubizek later recalled, "Words burst from him like a backed-up flood breaking through crumbling dams. In grandiose, compelling images, he sketched his future and that of his people." Hitler later told him, "It began at that hour."

In time, Hitler would extol Wagner as "the greatest prophetic figure the German people has had." Wagner's music and writings inflamed Hitler's imagination and fanned his hatred of Jews. Wagner wrote, "This hatred is as necessary to my nature as gall is to blood." The histrionics of Wagner's operas stirred Hitler to envision huge public extravaganzas. And he drew elements of his theories about Germans constituting an Aryan "master race" from Wagner's dramatic retelling of Nordic myths.

Hitler traveled to Vienna, where he wandered the streets for two weeks, attended opulent theatrical productions, and decided to seriously pursue his desire to paint. He applied for admission to the Viennese Academy of Fine Arts but he was rejected—twice. As he would later write, "I was so convinced that I would be successful that when I received my rejection, it struck me as a bolt from the blue." Hitler received a more devastating blow with the news that his mother, long suffering from breast cancer, had died on December 21, 1907.

Over the next six years, Hitler eked out a living in Vienna, earning paltry sums turning out postcard-sized water-color paintings. He lived in a flophouse for a time. His principal diversions were studying architecture and reading. He became known as a vigorous debater of politics and was a regular reader of the *Deutsches Volksblatt*, an anti-Semitic newspaper. He greatly admired Karl Lueger, the anti-Semitic mayor of Vienna, and became an especially strong critic of Social Democrats, the "Reds," and Jesuits.

In May 1913, Hitler moved to Munich, where he continued to sell paintings, work as a house painter, and voraciously read books on Marxism, a philosophy and economic practice he called a "world plague." When World War I broke out in the summer of 1914 (the United States would not enter the conflict until 1917), Hitler enlisted. "I fell down on my knees and thanked Heaven from an overflowing heart for granting me the good fortune of being permitted to live at this time," he later wrote.

He fought with the Bavarian Infantry and was promoted to corporal, serving as a dispatch runner, a particularly dangerous assignment. Hitler was wounded in the leg by a shell fragment in October 1916 and returned to battle after he recuperated. Two years later, shortly before the war's end, he was temporarily blinded by mustard gas. He was awarded the Iron Cross, Second Class, and the Iron Cross, First Class.

For this young man, Germany's defeat in World War I was nothing less than a humiliating national tragedy. In his autobiography, *Mein Kampf* ("My Struggle"), he lamented: "And so it had all been in vain ... Did all this happen only so that a gang of wretched criminals could lay hands on the father-land?... In those nights hatred grew in me, hatred for those responsible for this deed."

He blamed a vast array of people — including German Communists, Socialists, and Jews — for the country's disgrace. He excoriated the Allies as unjust in promulgating the punitive terms of the 1919 Versailles Treaty. He was particularly outraged that the treaty stipulated that Germany alone bore responsibility for World War I and thus was solely responsible for reparations for civilian losses.

The treaty also demanded that the country be demilitarized, capping its army at one hundred thousand men and limiting the navy to fifteen thousand personnel. Germany also was required to cede its overseas colonies and a number of territories in Europe. Manufacture or possession of certain munitions and weaponry was barred. The treaty also forbade Germany from creating a union with Austria.

These demands greatly rankled Hitler and many other Germans. U.S. President Woodrow Wilson worried that in time the harsh treatment of Germany might precipitate another European conflict far worse than the Great War of 1914 – 1918, because advances in weaponry assured many more deaths.

Speaking in Omaha, Nebraska, in September 1918, Wilson had warned, "I can predict with absolute certainty that within another generation, there will be another world war if the nations of the world do not concert the methods by which to prevent it."

A few days later, Wilson told a crowd in San Diego, California, "I do not hesitate to say that the war we have just been through, though it was shot through with terror of every kind, is not to be compared with the war we would have to face the next time. What the Germans used were toys as compared with what would be used in the next war."

By the early 1920s, the lack of political, economic, and social stability created a void for Hitler to seek power. He began casting a mesmerizing patriotic vision for the restoration of the German people — what he believed was their rightful place as the superior Aryan master race within the world order.

He was not the only German with such ideas. In 1918 in Munich, Anton Drexler formed a branch of the Free Committee for German Workers' Peace, and, a year later, he created the German Workers' Party, a group opposed to Communists and Social Democrats. He urged Germans to unite in a national community of one people — with no Jews allowed. Adolf Hitler was its fifty-fifth member.

The group soon changed its name to the National Socialist German Workers' Party, and by July 1921 Hitler was its undisputed leader. The Nazi Party was born, with Hitler viewing himself as a "drummer" and "rallier" of a national movement.

The party's militia, whose members were often referred to as storm troopers or brown shirts, was founded that year. Initially, the members of this paramilitary organization were bouncers who protected Nazi meetings at beer halls. As enforcers, they often initiated and fought in brawls in those drinking halls and in the streets of Munich where steins flew, shots were fired, and punches thrown. The organization became a loyal and ferocious force that embraced violence to accomplish the Nazi Party's goals.

On November 8, 1923, Hitler tried to seize power in the German state of Bavaria in what became known as the Beer Hall Putsch. At 8:30 p.m., Hitler and his storm troopers entered the Bürgerbräukeller, which was crammed with three thousand people. Hitler climbed on a chair, fired a pistol shot into the ceiling, and announced that he was forming a provisional government and that "a national revolution had begun."

It was short-lived. The next day when Hitler and two thousand supporters attempted to march to the Bavarian War Ministry, government soldiers and police confronted them. Hitler was in the first row when a shot rang out. In the ensuing thirty-second gun battle, fourteen of Hitler's supporters and four policemen were killed. The gunfire narrowly missed Hitler, but his shoulder was dislocated in the melee.

Arrested and convicted of treason in April 1924, Hitler was sent to Landsberg Prison, located in Landsberg am Lech, to serve a five-year prison term. And the Nazi Party was banned.

Hitler settled into prison life and, by the account of the governor of the prison, was obedient, quiet, and got along with fellow prisoners. He spent most of his waking hours writing *Mein Kampf.*

Just eight months later, in December 1924, Hitler's sentence was reduced and he walked out of prison. Despite the ban on the party, Hitler quickly reorganized it and created the SS as his own personal guard unit.

The Nazis competed in various national elections but gathered little popular support. As late as 1928, their candidates received only 3 percent of the national vote. At the time, Germans were fairly content with the status quo, particularly since the economy was prospering. But the Wall Street stock market crash of 1929 in the United States devastated the world's financial system. Hitler and the Nazis capitalized on this by blaming their political opponents for the scarcity of goods and the loss of jobs.

Germans were drawn more intently to Hitler's patriotic speeches and became captivated by his rhetorical skill, as he targeted Jewish financiers as the leading culprits in the collapse. By the tens of thousands, they began attending Nazi political rallies and marches. Their hearts pounded listening to beating drums as Nazi flags adorned with swastikas were hoisted high and they responded with the Nazi salute.

Hitler portrayed himself as one of them: an ordinary man who had suffered hardship and who loved boys and girls and dogs, and who found strength and renewal in his walks along Bavarian mountain trails. German citizens began to see Hitler as a potential savior, a man who could pull the nation out of its economic morass and restore the country to its rightful place as a leader of the world.

As Hitler's popularity surged, so did the ranks of the Nazi Party. In the 1930 elections, Nazi candidates won 18.3 percent of the vote. In 1932, Hitler ran for the German presidency and forced a run-off election with incumbent Paul von Hindenburg. Hitler was trounced — receiving 36.8 percent of the vote to von Hindenburg's 53 percent. The Nazi Party won 230 of the 608 seats in the legislature.

It was a hollow victory for von Hindenburg. In January 1933, unable to repair Germany's serious economic troubles and threatened by the rising influence of the Nazi Party, von Hindenburg acceded to Hitler's demand that Hitler become Germany's Chancellor.

Some people were deeply troubled by this decision, including von Hindenburg's one-time military colleague Erich Ludendorff, who warned the president in a telegram that he had just "handed over our sacred German Fatherland to one of the greatest demagogues of all time. I prophesy to you this evil man will plunge our Reich into the abyss and will inflict immeasurable woe on our nation."

Hitler's appointment was celebrated with a massive torchlight parade that lasted deep into the night of January 30, 1933, and, some claimed, was attended by one million marchers. Emboldened, Hitler almost immediately called for dissolution of the current government and for new legislative elections with an eye toward suppressing all political critics, whether Communists, Socialists, or members of other parties. He orchestrated approval of the Reichstag Fire Decree, a draconian measure that essentially stripped Germans of their civil rights. The law placed restrictions on personal liberty, on the right of free expression of opinion, including freedom of the press; on the rights of assembly and association; and on the privacy of postal, telegraphic, and telephonic communications. Warrants for house searches, orders for confiscations, as well as restrictions on who could own property, were legalized.

Under the decree, armed individuals who engaged in serious disturbances of the peace could be executed. Storm troopers were given arrest power and began scouring Germany in trucks, rousting and arresting Communists, Social Democrats, and Liberals. Many were tortured. Politicians who sought to speak out against Hitler frequently had their meetings shut down.

On March 3, 1933, Hitler's friend and ally Hermann Goering —he had been wounded in the Beer Hall Putsch in 1923 while marching with Hitler—let loose a tirade of threats against Hitler's opponents in Frankfort: "Fellow Germans, my measures will not be crippled by any judicial thinking ... I don't have to worry about justice; my mission is only to destroy and exterminate—nothing more!" He promised to lead the brown shirts against Communists and anyone who would oppose the Nazis.

International observers were clearly alarmed by the ferocity of the Nazis' tactics. Residents fleeing Germany spoke of being warned that their lives were in peril if they stayed.

In the elections that Hitler demanded, the Nazi Party received only 43.9 percent of the vote but managed to acquire a majority in the new legislature by forming a coalition with the Nationalists, who had garnered 8 percent of the vote.

Chancellor Hitler pressed von Hindenburg to endorse the Enabling Act, which would effectively give the cabinet, which Hitler controlled, the authority to enact laws that did not have to conform to the nation's constitution. If it passed, the cabinet would not need the approval of the Reichstag for four years.

On March 23, 1933, Hitler addressed the Reichstag and urged passage of the act. He claimed that strong leadership from the cabinet was needed if Germany was to be protected from its enemies. He promised that the government would "make use of those powers only insofar as they are essential for carrying out vitally necessary measures."

Though raised a Roman Catholic, Hitler had long before stopped practicing and some think that what religious beliefs he had were based more in paganism than Christianity. Yet he went out of his way to praise Christianity and won over some members of the Center Party, particularly after he suggested he would protect the civil and religious rights of Roman Catholics.

As Hitler spoke to the legislature, SS troops demonstrated outside, chanting loudly, "Full powers or else!"

The Enabling Act passed, 441 to 84. Intoxicated by their victory, Nazi legislators rose to their feet and lustily sang the party's anthem. The same day, the *Völkischer Beobachter*, a Nazi Party newspaper, published a chilling announcement: "On Wednesday the first concentration camp for 5,000 people will be set up near Dachau."

Heinrich Himmler, the future chief of the SS and then head of the Munich police force, had ordered the camp's creation. The first prisoners were to be Communists and Social Democrats.

On August 2, 1934, von Hindenburg died at age eighty-seven. Almost simultaneously, the cabinet consolidated the positions of chancellor and president and the title of president was erased. Hitler was *fuehrer* and *reich chancellor*. All members of the German military were obliged to take an oath swearing unconditional obedience to Hitler and to be prepared to risk their lives for him.

His rise to power had been swift and stunning. As the *New York Times* later declared: "Hitler was nothing, and from nothing he became everything to most Germans ... Sixty-five million Germans yielded to the blandishments and magnetism of this slender man of medium height, with little black mustache and shock of dark hair, whose fervor and demagogy swept everything before him with outstretched arms as the savior and regenerator of the Fatherland."

Immediately, Hitler turned his full attention to the building of a Third Reich, a *reich* he fervently believed was destined to last for one thousand years.

CHAPTER 3

TEEN PALM STEPPED OFF THE TRAIN IN RALEIGH, GREETED by a muggy August evening in 1933. He looked relatively fresh in his suit and tie, though he had been on the train for nearly a day. He had been driven by a friend to New York City's Grand Central station, boarded in darkness, and then watched as five hundred miles of lovely countryside rolled across the window — New Jersey — Delaware — Maryland — Virginia — until he was farther from home than he had ever been.

Clutching a suitcase in one hand and his saxophone case in the other, he scanned the platform. He had been expecting a greeting party, Jimmy Poyner and his "boys." But he saw no one until he spotted, far down the platform, a disheveled-looking man getting off the train. The man was immediately surrounded by a group of five younger men who had emerged from the station. One member of this crowd spotted Teen, and in a moment he and the rest of the young men were sprinting toward him.

The first to reach him thrust out his right hand and shouted, "Teen! Teen Palm! It's you!"

Teen nodded, reflexively dropped his suitcase and extended his right hand to grip the man's hand. "That's me," he said. "I'm Teen Palm."

"I'm Jimmy Poyner," the man said, continuing to pump his hand. "These boys are part of our band. We're so glad to meet you."

Teen's face broke into a broad grin as he said, "Well, hello to you, Jimmy. Boys. I'm so glad to be here."

After a quick round of introductions, Teen's suitcase and saxophone were scooped up and carried to a car parked behind the station.

"Sorry we weren't at your train car door when you got off," Poyner said. "But we saw this man carrying something that looked like a saxophone case and right away we thought it was you. But he wasn't — he was some kind of salesman — and then we saw you and, and ... So, welcome to Raleigh."

As the car sped off, Poyner continued his nonstop chatter: "We're heading straight down to Southern Pines where we practice. Is that okay? Of course it's okay, right? You can give us a listen, and then we want to hear you play that sax of yours and sing some of your favorite tunes."

Earlier that month, Teen had made his decision, telling his parents that he wanted to enroll at North Carolina State College. But instead of playing collegiate football, he wanted to try out for Poyner's "Southern Pines Orchestra." His parents gave him their reluctant blessing, never expressing to him their shared worry about where they were going to find the money; they were already paying tuition plus room and board for Teen's older brother at the school.

They were pleased, though, that Teen wouldn't be risking injury by playing football, and Susan was confident that his playing and singing would improve in a professional orchestra, believing that being in a working band might not only help cover the cost of his education but could lead to a show business career.

Crowded in a sedan, Poyner and the "boys" whisked Teen the seventy miles south to Southern Pines, where the band had summer living quarters. Even though it was late, they got right to business, and Teen was impressed as the band ran through a few numbers.

"Now, let's hear what you've got," said Poyner.

Teen played with passion and precision, and his audition was a success. He had a hard time determining whether he felt more elated or relieved when told he had been accepted into the band.

Poyner was so pleased with Teen's performance that he quickly arranged for him to sing on a Raleigh radio station for eight dollars a week. Back home in Mount Vernon, his parents and Aunt Nan were so excited by this news that they started asking friends if any had more powerful radios on which they might be able to hear Teen.

The days passed quickly as the band members spent long hours in rehearsal. Poyner and his younger brother, George, decided to rename the orchestra Jimmy Poyner's Famous Collegians and to hit the road, even though all of them had started classes at their respective colleges. With Teen as lead singer and featured saxophone player, the band quickly became popular as it toured the East Coast, playing on university campuses and in hotels and clubs.

This was the beginning of a productive and exciting period. Jimmy Poyner would later reminisce about it, writing:

During the four years we all played together — fourteen men, none of whom drank and only seven of whom smoked — we got along amazingly well as we travelled considerably between Washington, D.C., and Savannah, Georgia, and went to school in between. We never missed a day of playing in

*the four summers we worked, and we averaged three to five
nights a week during the winter. The fact that we got along
so well under these circumstances is to a great extent due to
Teen Palm's presence as he was extremely liked by all, never
displayed any temper, and was a great motivating force. With
his looks and voice, he captivated audiences all over this part
of the country.*

For a time, one band member was Les Brown, a student at
Duke University and later the leader of the immensely popular Les Brown and His Band of Renown. Brown arranged
much of the band's music and was particularly fond of Teen.

Even with the success of the band, Teen battled self-doubt
throughout his college years, worrying about his class work,
fearing that he was a drain on the family's finances, wondering whether he would be an utter disappointment, a failure.

Money was a frequent topic in letters from his mother, who
wrote in the fall of 1933:

Dearest Boys,

*I am enclosing a check to Cliff for $20 — a dollar more,
Cliff, than you said you'd need. So if Teen needs a few cents,
just divide with him and please don't be discouraged with your
mother if she is slow to understand where money goes. I have
quite a bit just now to shoulder and no one to help me — so
just bear up until I get myself together.*

*Now please write each week. My mind gets so upset. I
have terrible dreams of you and it's upsetting.*

*Loads of love to you both.
Your Devoted Mother*

Fred was working infrequently, and Susan relied on boarders and some sewing to make ends meet. Her letters to Teen

and Cliff invariably mentioned the difficulties she faced trying to keep the household afloat and how the hard economic times were making it difficult for many people in Mount Vernon. Frequently, she wondered where Cliff and Teen were spending the money she sent them and what Teen earned with the band. Little seemed to be applied to room and board.

Aunt Nan also wrote to Teen, offering him all manner of counsel regarding how to care for his health and baby his singing voice: "Keep your system open by taking something once a week. Chew a Fenemint or eat a Boll Rolls on Saturday nite. Every ailment comes from poison in the system."

Teen's sister, Gladys, kept Teen current about home life, friends, and local events in Mount Vernon. Always an encouraging voice, she predicted that someday he would be a national singing star. She loved a song he had composed and hoped it would be published.

In his sophomore year, after being accepted into Pi Kappa Phi, Teen lived in the campus fraternity house. In December 1934, the fraternity treasurer wrote his mother to report that he had failed to pay his initiation fee from the previous year and that he was two months behind on rent: "Embarrassing for both Teen and us."

Somehow, though, those bills and others got paid, and the 1936 college yearbook featured a photograph of Teen holding a pipe and sitting in a bathtub at the fraternity house. In another, he was shown lying on his bed reading a book and formally clad in a suit, white shirt, tie, and shoes.

But Teen expressed his lingering insecurities in a letter to his sister, written after a concert in the late summer of 1936:

It's about two AM and I'm whipped down. I want to get this off to you so it will leave on the early train. This is sort of an

apology concerning your birthday. I am sorry that I let the
24ᵗʰ go by without sending you a card or even some sort of
congratulations. It has gotten so that I don't even know what
day it is and the date doesn't enter my mind. We live from day
to day in music and as far as time goes we only check from
ten till one each night.

You probably think me pretty sorry after the swell things
you have done for me through all my twenty-three years.
I guess I am a washout as far as things of importance are
concerned. I hope I can make up for it in some manner or
form but I still can say happy birthday if it is not too late.

I hope you can make all of this out because I can't even see
or think.

All my love

In 1937, the band published a promotional brochure that singled out Teen for garnering "wide recognition with his song writing" and singing of "sweet vocals." The brochure included a photograph of the orchestra and in the lower right a showcase inset photograph of Teen. The brochure copy included this: "With increasing popularity and a reputation for entertainment and fine music which is now known throughout the East, this young organization has played major engagements in practically every city from Charleston, S.C., to Washington, D.C."

Teen was becoming increasingly convinced that he was on the threshold of a successful show business career. Poyner was always touting Teen as the best young band singer in the country, and he too saw big things in the future for his young singer and, in turn, for the band.

But then George Poyner was diagnosed with leukemia. Within months, he was dead. His brother was devastated, as were the rest of the band members. The group fell into disarray, and the future that had appeared so promising now was clouded in pain and uncertainty.

Despite his own brush with death in the car crash, or perhaps because of it, Teen was still young enough to feel indestructible. But now, for the first time, in the wake of George's death, and with fewer band performances to distract him from the tragedy, Teen was forced to confront the details of his life. It was not a pretty picture. His grades, never sterling, were worse in college; his most recent set of marks was pocked with more Ds than Cs, and nothing higher. There was justifiable fear that he would not be able to graduate in four years. And his financial world was marred with debts.

Compounding these troubles in the spring of 1937, a recurring pain in his abdomen that he had tried to ignore for nearly a year turned into a medical emergency. While traveling with the band near Burlington, N.C., his appendix burst. He was hospitalized for several days after surgery, and his physician later told Teen's mother that while the infection had spread to his large intestine, it had been stopped.

He noted, "I believe that Teen's health will be much better now than it has been as we found a stone in the appendix, the only one, incidentally, that I have ever seen. It well accounts for the nagging pain that has been troubling him for the past year or more."

George Poyner's death and Teen's physical problems, poor grades, failing finances, and ever-present self-doubt were a heavy load for Teen, and after much soul-searching he decided on a bold course. He dropped out of the orchestra, left college, and began to look for a steady job.

Jimmy Poyner never really got over his brother's premature

death. Not long afterward, he disbanded the orchestra and enrolled in law school. When Teen learned of this, it reassured him that his own decision had been the right one, even if he had no idea where it was going to lead.

CHAPTER 4

NESTLED IN ROLLING HILLS AND RINGED BY CLEAR, COLD trout streams, Salisbury, North Carolina, was very much a Southern city in 1937 when Charles J. Woodbridge arrived to become pastor of the First Presbyterian Church.

Settled by Scotch-Irish pioneers who traveled 450 miles by wagon from Pennsylvania to establish homes on the Yadkin River in Rowan County in 1753, Salisbury had a rich and often dark history. Daniel Boone was dispatched from there to explore Kentucky. Andrew Jackson studied law there.

During the Civil War, or the War of Northern Aggression, as some there called it, Salisbury was the site of a Confederate prisoner-of-war camp. Built for two thousand prisoners, it once housed up to ten thousand men living under ghastly conditions. Many did not survive their brutal incarceration —more than five thousand unidentified Union soldiers were buried in unmarked graves outside the prison walls. In August 1865, four months after the war, Union General George Stoneman burned it to the ground.

By 1930, the city had seventeen thousand residents, and most of them believed that Salisbury's attractive tree-lined streets, well-manicured Fulton Street residential district, accessible downtown with many stores, numerous churches, good schools, and well-manicured parks made an ideal place to live and work.

When Woodbridge and his family arrived, whites constituted the town's privileged majority. The Salisbury Railway Passenger Station reflected the social mores of that time and place. Black Americans had no choice but to enter the general waiting room through a different door than the one used by whites; ironically, nearly eighty years earlier, a group of locals had promoted a number of civic resolutions that included calling for the abolishment of the African slave trade. But in 1930, restrooms were segregated, and on the train, black Americans were forced to ride in cars at the front, where they suffered much stronger doses of soot and noise from the steam engines than did cars at the back of the train reserved for whites.

The station was an important stop on the railway line between Atlanta, Georgia, and Washington, D.C. In 1945, after Franklin Roosevelt died, hundreds of residents arose in the predawn darkness to line the railroad tracks and pack the station to view the president's funeral train as it made its way north from Warm Springs, Georgia, to Washington, D.C.

Many of Salisbury's young women embraced "white-glove" Southern etiquette. They dated under the watchful eye of chaperones and carefully heeded curfews. They followed traditional customs for "debutante," or coming-out, parties. Few young ladies considered professional careers or aspired to run businesses. Nevertheless, women often exercised considerable influence over the community's social life through their participation in clubs, civic organizations, school boards, and church activities.

As in much of America, the town's economy was mired in the Depression and feeling its effects in various ways. African Americans were moving northward in droves to industrial cities in the North and to the farms of California in search of work. For every antebellum mansion there were scores of sharecropper shacks. For a time, banks across the nation were failing at the rate of more than one per day. After the stock market crash in 1929, the annual gross national product dropped precipitously, and farm income dropped by more than half. In 1933, one out of four workers was unemployed. President Roosevelt instituted the first of his "Fireside Chats" in 1933 to try to assure Americans that the nation would recover and to encourage them to support his New Deal measures. It was a time when many were haunted by moral and spiritual doubts.

Like the original pioneers who had settled Salisbury, Charles Woodbridge and his family journeyed from Pennsylvania, where, in 1930, he had married Ruth Dunning, the daughter of Smith Gardner Dunning and his wife, Agnes. From 1929 to 1941, Smith Gardner Dunning was the pastor of Beulah Presbyterian Church in Churchill, Pennsylvania. Woodbridge traced his ancestors back to John Woodbridge, a fifteenth-century Lollard preacher in England. The Lollards were followers of the Oxford scholar and pre-Reformation theologian John Wycliffe, who spearheaded the first translation of the Latin Vulgate Bible into English. Since then, a Woodbridge in every generation had been a minister.

Charles was born in China in 1902, the son of Presbyterian missionaries. His mother, Jeanie Wilson Woodrow Woodbridge was a first cousin to Woodrow Wilson, the twenty-eighth president of the United States. In fact, Jeanie had reintroduced Wilson to her best friend, Ellen Louise Axon, the daughter of a Presbyterian minister. Ellen Louise Axon became Woodrow Wilson's first wife.

Woodbridge worked his way through Princeton University,

earning undergraduate and graduate degrees there. He was an all-American soccer player, holding his own against bigger and stronger foes by drawing on his expertise learned from the English children he had played with while in school in China. He earned a theological degree from Princeton Seminary and was ordained in 1927.

He first served the First Presbyterian Church in Flushing, New York, where he established a reputation as a hard-working clergyman with an outgoing personality who was interested in the lives of his church members. Athletic and vivacious, he endeared himself to others with a finely tuned blend of preaching within church walls and an avuncular sense of humor beyond the pulpit. Much of his ministry here was devoted to house-to-house visitation, and he met his goal of one thousand visits per year.

In 1932, he felt a call to become a missionary. This was not surprising. His father, the Rev. Samuel I. Woodbridge, had been a missionary in China and was the editor of the largest English-language religious newspaper in that country, the *Chinese Christian Intelligencer.* Not only had Charles Woodbridge been raised as an intellectual — he was a Phi Beta Kappa scholar at Princeton; knew Hebrew, Greek, Latin, French, and German; and had studied under some of the greatest theologians of the time, including Adolf von Harnack — he was schooled to have an appreciation for and understanding of the global community.

Samuel Woodbridge, his father, exchanged correspondence with and provided counsel to President Wilson. In a September 1914 letter to Samuel, Wilson expressed his personal anguish over the outbreak of World War I, although the U.S. did not declare war on Germany until 1917:

My dear Cousin:

I cannot send you an adequate reply to your generous letter of August fifteenth which has touched me very much. I can only say how fully I realize your power to sympathize with me in my present darkness and distress and how sincerely obliged I am for the voice of sympathy and of comfort which comes to me with your letter.

We think of you very often, particularly in the present extraordinary circumstances of the world, and I hope things are going as well with you as it is possible for them to go in these circumstances, and, besides, that you are well.

Cordially and sincerely yours,
Woodrow Wilson

Presbyterians had long been active in missionary work around the globe, and Ruth Woodbridge had spent three years in French Cameroon, West Africa, teaching the children of missionaries. She returned to the United States, where she met Charles on a blind date at a dinner party in New York City. They were married on March 4, 1930, by Ruth's father in his church in Churchill, Pennsylvania. In June 1932, Charles, Ruth, and their one-year-old daughter, Norma Jean, embarked again for West Africa. *Time* magazine featured a photograph of the three in its religion section.

Their stay was brief. In September of 1934, Woodbridge accepted an invitation to go to Philadelphia to become the secretary general of the newly constituted Independent Presbyterian Board for Foreign Missions that was founded by Dr. J. Gresham Machen, a renowned theologian and former professor at Princeton Theological Seminary. But that decision turned disastrous when a dispute broke out among some church officials who saw the board as a direct challenge to their authority to control the foreign missions program of their church. Machen was put on trial by an ecclesiastical court and suspended from the exercise of his ministerial functions by the Northern Presbyterian Church. A disheartened Woodbridge suffered the same fate.

When the call came from the First Presbyterian Church of Salisbury, Woodbridge saw it as an opportunity to start anew. His father had been a Southern Presbyterian, so he saw going to Salisbury as a return to his family roots.

The church had been founded in 1821 and was a town landmark, its bell tower facing Innes Street. The family moved into the church's two-story brick manse on the corner across the street. On many evenings, the family gathered to read and relax on the veranda flanked by Doric columns.

In the living room hung a portrait of Maxwell Chambers and his wife, Catherine, both of whom had wielded enormous financial influence in the church. After their deaths in the 1850s, they were buried under what later became the lecture room in the church. Along with gifts of money and property, the Chamberses had stipulated in their wills that a religious service be held once a month on the floor above their graves.

Woodbridge was a dynamic speaker who loved to preach and teach the Bible. A clear and gifted communicator, he carefully outlined each sermon in a manner that listeners could easily follow. In 1938, he was invited to be a guest speaker for a week of meetings at the Independent Presbyterian Church in Savannah as part of a revival campaign. The *Historians Report*, a publication of the church, noted that he exuded "great personal charm, a brilliant mind, and keen understanding." Those characteristics were on full display in Salisbury and church members — particularly young men and women — embraced him enthusiastically.

In 1938, a Sunday school room was opened and more pews were added as the congregation began to swell. Woodbridge organized a volunteer choir whose ranks were soon populated with talented singers from nearby Catawba College.

He developed close personal ties with a number of his parishioners, many of whom were influential citizens such as Charlie Burkett, Salisbury's fire chief, and Ross Garrison, the assistant fire chief and town barber, who, according to Woodbridge, "knew all the Salisbury gossip." More than once during church services, the town fire alarm would sound, Burkett and Garrison would bolt out the door, and Woodbridge would immediately stop preaching in order to pray for those whose lives might be in danger.

Woodbridge also became a part of the social fabric of the town, participating in all manner of non-church activities, such as goose hunting with Harry Frymoyer, a sergeant of the state police, and Sheriff Jim Krider. On one occasion, Krider invited Woodbridge to accompany him on his evening patrol, saying, "Pastor, then you will know how your church members really live."

Woodbridge would later recall one of those spine-tingling night rides: "Krider drove like Jehu [a biblical commander of chariots] for several miles in pursuit of a drunk culprit who drove head-on into a garden wall, was unharmed, and turned out to be one of my more docile members!" The parishioner was likely mortified to see his pastor sitting next to the sheriff in the police car.

In October 1939, Woodbridge began teaching a Bible class, which quickly became popular among the city's young men. Though nearing forty, Woodbridge was filled with an appealing youthful energy. He was clearly a man of God, but with his familiar manner, contagious sense of humor, and worldly intelligence, he easily related to young people, even those who were not particularly godly or spiritual. Townspeople of Salisbury who did not normally attend the First Presbyterian Church began to receive invitations from their friends to join them and hear the pastor preach.

One person to receive such an invitation was Teen Palm.

CHAPTER 5

BY 1935, WITH HITLER FULLY IN CONTROL OF GERMANY, HIS long-simmering hatred of Jews began to surface more publicly. Although fewer than 1 percent of Germany's fifty-five million residents were Jewish, Hitler announced at the annual Nuremberg Rally in September a law with restrictive provisions aimed directly at Jews, including barring marriage to Germans. Violations were punishable by hard labor or prison.

In his speech, Hitler said the laws were designed to "achieve the legislative regulation of a problem which, if it breaks down again, will then have to be transferred by law to the National Socialist Party for final solution."

Millions of words have been written about Hitler, charting the course of his life and trying to explain his inherent evil, to dissect the monster within the man. Still, it is important here to recall some of the basics and how he began to focus on building the country's military might and establishing himself as a force on the world's geopolitical stage.

He instituted a military draft and boosted the German Army to five hundred fifty thousand men, two acts that were in direct violation of the Treaty of Versailles signed by Germany after World War I. The treaty had required that Germany give up considerable portions of its territory, pay financial reparations, and reduce the size of its military. Under the treaty, the area known as the Rhineland — the industrial heart of the nation, an area that stretched to the border with France — became a demilitarized zone overseen by Great Britain and France.

Despite Hitler's violations of the treaty, there was no reaction from the rest of the world. Still, just to reassure potential opponents, Hitler, in a speech at the German legislature, said, "Our love of peace perhaps is greater than in the case of others, for we have suffered most from war. None of us wants to threaten anybody, but we all are determined to obtain the security and equality of our people."

He promised Germany would honor all other provisions of the Treaty of Versailles and vowed to cooperate in maintaining peace in Europe. But in March 1936, Hitler violated the treaty again when he sent three German Army battalions across the Rhine River into Rhineland. When he announced this action at the German legislature, the lawmakers leaped to their feet and began to cheer him, with shouts of "Heil!"

Again, the rest of the world was silent. The French did nothing. Neither did the British.

Weeks later, in a nationwide referendum, virtually all registered voters went to the polls and nearly all of them voted to support Hitler's action. Emboldened again, he became determined to use that year's Summer Olympic Games in Berlin — awarded to Germany in 1931, before Hitler came to power — as a showcase for the nation and himself.

These games immediately became mired in controversy after non-Aryans were banned from Germany's team. After the Nazis agreed to let foreign Jews take part, the U.S. Amateur Athletic Union barely approved a measure to participate. While Hitler had hoped the games would prove a testament to Aryan superiority—and indeed the Germans did best the Americans in the overall medal count, eight-nine to fifty-six —Jesse Owens, a black American, stole much of the limelight by winning four gold medals.

Still, the games were a public-relations success for Hitler and the Nazi Party. The media lavishly praised the games, and favorable reports poured in from tourists who attended. Not long after, a schoolteacher from Idaho spent several weeks traveling in Germany and filed dispatches that appeared in the local paper back home: "The whole country looked like the stage of an opera, with lovely, red, white and black Swastika flags everywhere. Every hour or so in Munich, a handsome group of magnificently uniformed soldiers came stepping around the corner in absolute precision and singing a rousing military song in perfect time to their march. Really, it was most exhilarating."

She felt fortunate to have obtained a ticket to the Bayreuth Wagner Festival. She marveled at "many of Europe's crown princes and politicians in tuxedoes, accompanied by women wearing the latest Parisian fashions enthusiastically saluting Hitler with 'Heil' as he stepped out of his Mercedes upon his arrival at the theater. They repeated this act of adoration once they saw him emerge in the balcony to take his seat for the performance."

She attended the German Art Festival in Munich and saw Hitler review a three-hour parade. "I felt like I was living in the days of ancient Rome while in Munich," she wrote. "For three nights, the big buildings of Munich had tremendous iron braziers atop each of them with fire shooting from them high into the sky.

"Everywhere I talked politics without getting into trouble and everywhere the Germans told me that they loved Hitler.

I refuse to believe that the Germans are completely controlled through fear. It is a lie. I have watched their faces when he comes in their midst. Their countenances are transfixed and they 'Heil, heil, heil, heil' over and over again with a worshipful attitude that would make anyone conclude that they are happy. He has brought order out of chaos."

Hitler strongly believed in the concept of *lebensraum*, a term coined in the twentieth century, which referred to the unification of the country and the acquisition of other countries. General Karl Ernst Haushofer, a geopolitics professor at the University of Munich who was well known to Hitler, claimed this idea justified the creation of an expansionist-minded Germany. Haushofer declared: "I intend to teach Political-Geography as a weapon to reawaken Germany to fulfill its destined greatness. I shall re-educate the whole nation to an awareness of the role of geography in history so that every young German shall cease to think parochially but think instead in terms of whole continents."

Haushofer believed that the Aryan race had originated in distant Asia. This justified extending Germany's land grab beyond Eastern Europe. Haushofer further argued that the nation that controlled the continental heartland of Eurasia could dominate the entire world. Whether he intended to do so or not, Haushofer armed Hitler with an intoxicating vision and rationale for Aryan world domination.

In *Mein Kampf*, Hitler wrote that the German people needed *lebensraum* to grow and prosper — even if it meant slaughtering others to take their land.

If anyone in Germany had any doubts about Hitler's plans, they were erased on February 4, 1938, when he assembled his cabinet and declared that he was personally taking over command of all German armed forces. Factories began to hum, producing weapons at breakneck speed. The nation was being indoctrinated that duty to Hitler was of paramount importance. By then the Treaty of Versailles was essentially worthless, trampled to bits.

Hitler went after Austria first. At dawn on Saturday, March 12, 1938, German soldiers in tanks and armored vehicles met no resistance as they rumbled into Austria.

Czechoslovakia was next. On Saturday, October 1, German soldiers and tanks shot into the Sudetenland, a portion of western Czechoslovakia occupied by about three million ethnic Germans. That led to the signing of the Munich Agreement by Germany, France, Britain, and Italy, which officially sanctioned the occupation of the Sudetenland.

British Prime Minister Neville Chamberlain, who signed the agreement, along with Italy's Benito Mussolini and French Prime Minister Edouard Daladier, considered it the beginning of a time of peace in Europe. Upon his return to England, Chamberlain told a crowd of supporters that the settlement of the Czechoslovakian problem was a "prelude to a larger settlement in which all Europe may find peace." He famously said, "I believe it is peace for our time." He was famously mistaken.

Three weeks after the agreement was signed, Hitler told his staff that their list of future tasks should include "the liquidation of the remainder of Czechoslovakia."

Up to this time, there had been little anti-Semitic violence in Germany. But in Vienna, Jews were being forced into humiliating labor such as cleaning public toilets. Thousands were jailed. The Nazis opened the first concentration camp outside Germany at Mauthausen, near Linz. Within weeks, Poland declared that it was withdrawing the passports of Polish citizens who had been abroad for more than five years. Faced with accepting more than fifteen thousand Polish

Jews, including more than two thousand children, the SS was ordered to send them to Poland with one night's notice. Allowed just one suitcase per person, the Jews were packed onto trains and sent to Poland. But the Polish government refused legal entry to more than half of them. They were forced into refugee camps at the border that quickly became hellholes of disease and death.

Among those ousted was the family of Herschel Grynszpan, a teenager who was studying in Paris at the time. When Grynszpan heard what had happened to his family, he bought a pistol, went into the German Embassy in Paris, and shot to death a junior member of the staff. Hitler used the incident as an excuse to launch violent attacks on Jews on November 9–10, 1938.

It was essentially the beginning of the Holocaust, and throughout Germany and Austria, mobs of Hitler youth, SS members, and storm troopers smashed windows and looted Jewish shops and department stores. Synagogues were attacked and set ablaze. Sacred Torah scrolls were pulled apart and burned. The attacks came to be known collectively as Kristallnacht, or the Night of Broken Glass. An estimated seven thousand five hundred Jewish businesses were destroyed. More than two hundred fifty synagogues were torched. A total of ninety-one Jews were reported murdered, and more than twenty-five thousand others were transported to concentration camps in Dachau, Buchenwald, and Sachsenhausen, where many of them were killed.

All doubt of Hitler's new power should have been erased on his fiftieth birthday on April 20, 1939, when the Nazis put on an extravaganza of military force unlike any ever seen.

The morning began with a serenade from an Army band as Hitler emerged in full dress uniform from the Chancellery, the seat of the German government, and stood at attention, his hands folded before him. He then led a parade of fifty limousines that slowly cruised down the Avenue of Splendor carrying representatives from many countries, including Italy, Japan, Spain, Hungary, Belgium, Bolivia, Brazil, Bulgaria, Denmark, Finland, Greece, Yugoslavia, Lithuania, the Netherlands, Norway, Romania, Sweden, Slovakia, and Siam. Their number did not include representatives of Britain, France, or the United States.

Massive crowds — men and women, the elderly, and young children — lined the street, and everywhere in the city, banners proclaimed Hitler a "Guardian of Peace." Storefronts were festooned with his photograph. One building bore a portrait two stories tall. Flags bearing swastikas fluttered from hundreds of balconies.

Shortly before noon, Hitler left his limousine and strode to a canopied reviewing stand. As he took a seat in a gilded chair covered in red upholstery and raised his arm in the Nazi salute, tens of thousands of enthralled onlookers raised their arms and roared, "Seig heil!"

Their voices were nearly drowned out when more than 160 fighter planes thundered overhead in formation. Hitler stared straight ahead, his hand outstretched, as the first of forty thousand — soldiers, sailors, paratroopers, and airmen — began goose-stepping past the reviewing stand. Tanks rumbled down the avenue. There was a steady stream of fire- and manpower — troop transport trucks, horse-drawn cannons, antiaircraft guns, motorcycles with sidecars, and jeeps — along with every type of military equipment imaginable.

Flatbed semitrucks lumbered past, hauling massive artillery never seen publicly before. One cannon was so large that four trucks were required to carry its disassembled parts.

The parade lasted more than four hours.

Afterward, Hitler moved on to the Chancellery, the building that housed the many gifts that had begun arriving days earlier. Scores of presents were laid out on tables in the massive main hall.

There were marble statues and Meissen porcelain. The Nazi Party gave him a collection of letters of Frederick the Great, the eighteenth century king of Prussia, which had been purchased in various parts of the world. Other gifts included original scores by Richard Wagner, Hitler's favorite composer. There were many oil portraits, including what was said to be Titian's *Venus with a Mirror* (questions would later arise about its authenticity). The tributes seemed unending: silver, antique weapons, tapestries, rare artifacts, and vases of flowers. There were dozens of cakes, some in the shape of tanks, and chocolate tarts neatly arranged in the shape of swastikas.

Perhaps the most spectacular gift, also from the Nazi Party, was a mountaintop chalet, called the Eagle's Nest. It was a lavishly built and furnished lodge atop a mountain that overlooked the Obersalzberg, a compound of eighty buildings in the Bavarian mountains near Berchtesgaden, southeast of Munich. This compound included a house for Hitler, the Berghof, as well as an underground bunker system, offices, meeting rooms, and government archives connected by four miles of tunnels. It would serve as Hitler's second seat of government and would one day be a focal point in a massive manhunt for the dictator.

Birthday greetings by the thousands poured in from across the country and abroad, from lowly and powerful people, all praising Hitler.

"I believe in God, protector of heaven and earth, and that he has chosen Adolf Hitler as his son to relieve his people of the brood of Jews — and their dynasties," read a letter from a hotel porter.

Another was even more direct: "I have no God but you and no gospel but your teachings."

Hitler's top aide, Field Marshal Hermann Goering, declared the dictator "the greatest German of all times." And Paul Goebbels, Hitler's chief propagandist, said Hitler's "name wanders around the earth almost like a legend."

By the summer of 1939, Hitler and the Nazis had taken over Czechoslovakia and began looking toward Poland. Now, he was prepared to go to war. His troops, he declared, must be ready and not falter.

"Close your hearts to pity!" Hitler ordered his soldiers. "Act brutally! Eighty million people must obtain what is their right. Their existence must be made secure."

The presents from his fiftieth birthday party had by then been packed away in various places. Among them was a case containing a semiautomatic pistol. It was gold-plated with ivory grips. Hitler's initials were inlaid with gold on the grip. The gun was a gift from Carl Walther, the scion of the family that made hundreds of thousands of weapons sold worldwide. An inscription on the right side of the barrel said the gun was made by the armament manufacturing company in the German city of Zella-Mehlis.

Hitler was familiar with guns and often carried one for protection. He prized this new pistol and kept it in his Munich apartment, neatly tucked into a drawer of the desk in his office.

CHAPTER 6

WITHIN DAYS OF THE ARRIVAL OF THE WOODBRIDGE FAMILY in Salisbury in 1937, Teen Palm moved to town to work for the Commercial Credit Company. He was twenty-four, handsome, and loaded with charm and considerable musical talent. He rarely missed an opportunity to attend a dance, usually with his saxophone case tucked under his arm so that he could indulge the frequent urge to take to the stage and commandeer the microphone to the delight of his new friends.

His showmanship was not confined to the evenings, as he began to fashion himself a "business entertainer" and could frequently be found on golf courses nurturing clients or wooing prospective ones. Over the next two years, he ably and enthusiastically played the role of the witty bachelor whose smile was quick and easy but not without a hint of mystery. Few disagreed with the sentiment of one young woman in Salisbury who referred to him as "the most handsome man in town."

Still, as he moved from party to party, and from the first tee to the eighteenth green, he also moved from job to job. It was almost as if he saw his career as merely a means to have an income that would allow him to sustain a lifestyle of entertainment, parties, and socializing. He lasted less than eighteen months at the credit company before jumping to Hardiman & Son Hardware Co. in the nearby town of Spencer.

Hardiman was the source of all manner of goods, from automobile tires and batteries to hammers, nails, wrenches, saws, paint, and bicycles. He also took a turn at the lone gasoline pump out front of the store, filling cars with fuel, polishing windshields, and checking the oil. Within a year, he changed jobs again, going to work in the Salisbury office of an automobile-financing company based in Raleigh.

Was he drifting? Or was he merely taking the opportunity of his youth and personality to live a life of comparative ease during a time of great financial strain across the nation?

In early 1939, the first of two events that would shape the rest of his life occurred when he and a friend went on a double date. It was a blind date for Teen and his pal, Jack Busby. Busby was paired with Helen Raney, and Teen was paired with Helen's roommate, Eunice Smith. But what began quite innocuously turned into something else. Raney was smitten, and so was Palm — but with each other, not their dates. Teen may not have realized it then, but he had found his soul mate.

Raney was almost three years older than Palm, born in 1910 in Faith, North Carolina, less than ten miles south of Salisbury. She had been raised in a simple, wholesome atmosphere on a farm where dinner plates were filled with the bounty of the family garden and her chores included feeding the pigs, gathering eggs, and picking cotton. Unlike Palm, she well knew the aching back that comes with a hard day's labor in the North Carolina heat and humidity.

Shortly after Helen's mother, Mary Rusher, was married, her husband, Baxter Raney, abandoned her and moved to West Virginia to take a railroad job. Mary, who was pregnant with Helen, moved back with her parents and two siblings, a brother and a sister. There Helen was born. Mary and Helen lived there until her mother eventually remarried and they moved into a place of their own. But life there was difficult for Helen — her education was sporadic at best, and after falling behind in school, Helen moved back in with her grandparents. Her grandmother, Ruth Ann Elizabeth Peeler Rusher, was a strong God-fearing matriarch, and she raised Helen like she had raised her own children — with a deep, abiding love and a strong sense of right and wrong. Ruth Ann was not reluctant to wield a switch now and again to rein in the unruly child.

Helen worked hard in school and ultimately excelled. She graduated Granite Quarry High School in 1930, earned a diploma in secretarial skills at the Salisbury Business School in 1931, and found a job at Leonard's Jewelry in Salisbury. The owner and his wife treated her like family. With her strong work ethic, a finely calibrated moral compass, and charismatic personality, Helen flourished. An attractive young woman, Helen was determined to make something of herself, not an easy task in that time and place.

Teen and Helen's courtship developed slowly, beginning with an anonymous Valentine's Day telegram he sent her on February 14, 1940.

Less than one thousand years ago, the heretofore mentioned day was founded. It certainly is strange how a peculiar oddity like this was handed down through the ages but it just goes to show you what humanity is made of. How-ever I want to take the same opportunity to wish you Happy Valentine's Day.

In July, the finance company sent Palm to Charlotte to work for several weeks. Writing on company stationery, he told Helen, "You really are swell to me and I want you to know how much it means if you don't already have an idea."

In September, Teen wrote again, saying that the song "Begin the Beguine" was playing on the radio as he wrote. As he would scores of times in the future, he referred to his letters to her as a chat. He promised to "drop in again via the postman from time to time. I hope the reading was as pleasant as the writing ..." He signed off, "Love and Kisses, Teen."

Later that month, Helen was hospitalized with diphtheria and Teen sent flowers. He had come to realize just how deeply Helen had invaded his heart. Helen always would believe that was a turning point in their relationship, for soon after, her suitor's letters became more direct.

A few days before Christmas, Teen wrote from Kannapolis, North Carolina, where he was attending a business meeting.

I've got you on my mind, sweetheart, and wanted to drop in via the postman for a little chat with you as it seems years since I saw you last.

Did I ever tell you that you had the most beautiful eyes and smile that I ever saw in my life? Did I ever tell you that I love you more than anything else in the world? That I miss you more and more as the clock ticks off the records of life? That you are the most wonderful episode that has ever happened in my life? That nothing could ever be anything worthwhile to me without you? That the paramount thing is just the two of us? That I will work my fingers to the bone to make you happy?

I love you

On December 30, Teen wrote to wish Helen a happy New Year and made his intention even clearer. He also broke the news that he had lost his job:

Dearest Sweetheart,

You are so wonderful and sweet and I love you with all my heart and soul. I am going to marry you right away, too. Think of that — You can't do anything about it — I've just lost my job, but I can still be real sweet. I am true blue to you. I love you.

About the same time Teen met Helen, a business associate of his invited him to the First Presbyterian Church to hear Charles Woodbridge teach the Bible. Teen was never much of a churchgoer, but he reluctantly accepted, attending an evening service where Woodbridge was teaching from the book of Revelation. Almost in spite of himself, he was captivated and began going to the morning Sunday school Bible class, where Woodbridge was teaching from the gospel of John. When the pastor reached the third chapter and the story of Nicodemus the Pharisee, it roused something deep in Teen's spirit.

Nicodemus was a member of the Jewish ruling party — the Pharisees — the group of men most adamantly opposed to Jesus's teachings. Nicodemus knew all about Jesus and what he taught. He was quite possibly a closet disciple.

In fact, when he finally sought Jesus out, it was secretly, in the middle of the night. Jesus told Nicodemus that in order to enter the Kingdom of God, he must be born again.

This was a new idea and a new term and it literally made no sense. Nicodemus's response to Jesus bordered on the sarcastic: "How can a man be born when he is old? Can he enter a second time into his mother's womb and be born?"

Jesus told Nicodemus that he wasn't talking about a physical rebirth. The born-again experience Jesus described was spiritual: "The wind blows where it wills, and you hear the sound of it, but you do not know whence it comes or whither it goes; so it is with everyone who is born of the Spirit."

Peering deep into his soul and heart, Teen realized that, like Nicodemus, he was not a living, breathing believer reborn of the spirit. As he later recalled in a personal account of those days, "I suddenly realized that I was not ready for Christ's coming, and if he were to come at that moment, I would be lost, a counterfeit, to be eternally cast out."

He invited Helen to join him at the church, and they both began studying the Bible. Although they both came from religious families — Teen's was Presbyterian, Helen's was Lutheran — both were essentially seekers looking for God. As a child, Teen attended Sunday school, and his mother regularly took the children to Sunday services, though his father never joined them. Helen's grandmother voraciously read the Bible. She planted seeds of faith, in fact, in Helen, though Helen would later refer to herself in those days as "religious, but lost."

If Teen had been asked if he were a Christian before he went to Salisbury, he would have nodded yes in intellectual assent. After all, he had gone to Sunday school, knew Bible stories, and was a decent, good person. But as Teen later explained, upon listening to Woodbridge teach the Gospel of John, he became persuaded that he needed a personal savior. He would speak of the power of the Holy Spirit that led him to confess his sins and invite Jesus to be Lord of his life.

For Teen, this experience of being born again gave him a genuine sense of joy, an assurance of his eternal destination, and the kind of peace the Bible says surpasses all understanding.

He was very eager to move forward in this new, born-again life with Helen at his side. They spoke of it in their letters that summer, when Helen went on vacation with girlfriends to Myrtle Beach, South Carolina. Teen wrote to her almost daily:

Dearest Sweetheart:

I miss you already and wish you were here. Take care of yourself and I'll pray for us each night ... Sweet Sweetheart, have a good time and remember that I miss you and love you with all my heart and soul. I'll be waiting only for Sunday as that will be a wonderful day with you by my side.

I just love you to pieces and will just keep on loving you more and more and more cause you are the sweetest Sweetheart of all.

Love and kisses

In reply, Helen wrote that she hoped to be back from Myrtle Beach by 7:00 a.m. Sunday so they could go to church together. She added, "I have been saying a nice prayer for us each day — but I haven't read the Bible. Bet you have though."

Woodbridge was thrilled with the couple's new commitment to Christ and invited Teen to join a small group of men who prayed each Sunday afternoon for the ministry of the church and their personal concerns. It was the beginning of a long and deep personal friendship between the two men.

As Teen and Helen turned to Christ, the eyes of the nation were increasingly turning toward Europe where the military and political situation was deteriorating rapidly. After negotiating an alliance with Italy's Benito Mussolini, Hitler invaded Poland on September 1, 1939. German forces, already in control in Austria and Czechoslovakia, swept into Denmark and Norway. Hitler signed a nonaggression treaty with the Soviet Union, and then, ominously, in September 1940, Japan joined the Axis with Germany and Italy.

Woodbridge occasionally interrupted his Bible teachings to speak about the war in Europe. His parishioners were deeply worried, and he realized they needed to hear words of comfort and hope — to be reassured God was in control of history and human events.

"We are living in unusual days," he declared one Sunday in May 1940. "The German eagle, which already clutches in its fierce talons Austria, Czechoslovakia, portions of Poland, Denmark, and Norway, has today entered Holland, Belgium, and Luxembourg. Armies are about to clash on a wide frontier ... Two ideologies, democracy and totalitarian might, are now facing each other in battle array on the field.

"No man knoweth the day or the hour," he preached. "But as we watch with mounting indignation the affairs abroad, let us be very sure that our own hearts are brimming with warm and tender love for the Lord Jesus. Let us never despair, for our Father doeth according to His will in the armies of heaven and among the inhabitants of earth."

The next month, France fell to Hitler's military onslaught.

Many of the townspeople of Salisbury turned to prayer, asking God to stay the hand of Hitler's armies, Navy, and Air Force, and to restore peace to Europe. The church elders designated a special day of "prayer and supplication to our Heavenly Father that he may intervene in the horrible struggles of war and peace may once more reign supreme in the hearts of men."

In August, the German Luftwaffe attacked England from the air, and the Battle for Britain was joined. Although President Franklin D. Roosevelt, campaigning for reelection against Wendell Wilkie, assured the nation's mothers and fathers that their boys were not going to be sent to fight in a foreign war unless the United States was attacked, that September he supported the passage of the Selective Service Act by Congress, establishing the military draft.

The military situation in Europe continued to spiral downward. On November 14, 1940, Coventry, England, experienced an especially terrifying round of firebombing from the Nazis. Roosevelt warned the nation in a speech on December 29, 1940, that "our civilization" was in great danger. He declared: "The Nazi masters of Germany have made it clear that they intend not only to dominate all life and thought in their own country, but also to enslave the whole of Europe, and then to use the resources of Europe to dominate the rest of the world." That same day, the Nazis unleashed a savage aerial onslaught of firebombs in an apparent attempt to burn London to the ground.

The winter and spring saw matters further worsen, but for Teen and Helen, the war remained distant and removed as they planned for their wedding.

It was a simple ceremony, performed June 7, 1941, in Helen's hometown of Faith in the living room of the Lutheran minister. Amidst baskets of lilies and white roses, the minister and his wife and a friend sang "O Perfect Love" and the couple exchanged vows. After a brief honeymoon trip to Virginia, they returned to Salisbury and their jobs — he at the auto finance company, she at Leonard's Jewelry. But a life that seemed perhaps idyllic and tranquil to the newlyweds did not last.

On the morning of December 7, 1941, after Teen and Helen attended adult Sunday school and the 11:00 a.m. church service, he went to his weekly men's prayer session. As a new believer, he enjoyed meeting with these men and Woodbridge for prayer and to get to know each other better. As they

[77]

dropped to their knees, a church member burst through the door.

"Pastor!" he exclaimed. "We've been attacked! Japanese planes have bombed Pearl Harbor! The battle is still going on!"

The next day, well before the American public would learn the full extent of the attack — more than two thousand men killed and the near destruction of the U.S. Navy — a somber President Roosevelt declared the bombing a "date that will live in infamy" and authorized a declaration of war on Japan.

Three days later, Germany and Italy declared war on the United States, and less than two months after that, Teen Palm was drafted by the U.S. Army. He was going to war.

CHAPTER 7

TEEN PALM WAS AMONG THE HUNDREDS OF MEN AND women from Salisbury going off to war, including nearly 150 from the First Presbyterian Church. In February, he boarded a train for Fort Jackson in Columbia, South Carolina, for basic training. His brother, Cliff, also was drafted and was dispatched to the Army Signal Corps.

Helen visited Teen his first weekend in Columbia, taking the bus there. The visit was too short, and they pledged to write each other every day. That Sunday night, after arriving home, Helen was true to her word. Sitting in bed, in her flowing longhand she wrote a note to her husband. Over the next six weeks, they wrote each other sometimes twice a day, and the letters flew back and forth between Salisbury and Fort Jackson.

Their letters spoke of packages, sent and received, of cookies, candy, writing paper, cold medicine, and a ChapStick for Teen when his lips were sunburned. There was news of births, deaths, weddings, steak dinners, and trips to the soda shop. In their letters, they declared their growing love for one another and their deepening faith in God. Teen wrote in the Service Club, in his tent, at the mess hall. Helen wrote at work, standing in the post office, perched on her couch, or, frequently, sitting in bed before falling asleep.

On March 3, Teen wrote:

Dearest Sweetheart,

The pictures, pen set and candy came along with your newsy letter. The pen set is swell and is just right for Army pocket wear. I am putting it in the bottom of my foot locker until I finish my training as I don't want to lose it on the drill field. You are such a wonderful sweetheart and so thoughtful and I just love you to pieces.

I feel like I have walked a thousand miles this past week, but am getting stronger in the legs so I can keep it up.

We got our rifles today. We now wear gas masks each day to get used to carrying them but we haven't pulled them from their cases for gas drill yet. I see that all of Salisbury will be equipped with gas masks soon. Take good care of yours as they tell us here the gas mask is the most important piece of equipment we have.

Before I go to bed, I want you to know that you are the sweetest sweetheart that ever was. I'm a lucky fellow.

They yearned to be together and lamented that they could not. On March 5, Helen wrote:

Dearest Sweetheart,

Today, three weeks ago, Uncle Sam took my sweetheart away and I miss him terribly. To tell you the truth, I wish Uncle Sam had a wife so he'd be a little more understanding. Darling, I love you so very good and I am so very glad Jesus gave you to me. As long as I know it's the will of our Savior, I suppose I just have to forgive Uncle Sam.

On March 10, Teen sent off an account of his day:

*We took a seven mile hike and practiced charging and small
war skirmishes. I just finished cleaning my rifle, washing my
mess kit and shining my shoes. I love you extra special all the
time. It will always be that way no matter how old we get. It's
wonderful to look ahead to the wonderful happiness we have
coming after this war is over. It's as plain as the nose on my
face because Jesus will never fail us. I feel it in my bones as if
he were telling me.*

They spoke by telephone twice a week, most frequently
on Sunday, setting up their call times by letters. If a call was
missed, there was great disappointment, but that paled compared with the news Teen delivered in his March 12 letter:

*I can't come home this weekend. I will call you Sunday at 3
p.m. I can talk for three minutes for 45 cents, which is half of
other days, so I guess that is the best time.*

*I got paid today—$8.40 which pays me through the end of
last month. On the 1st, I will start getting my full $21 and five
goes to you. Before I say goodnight, I want you to know that
you are just a wonderful sweetheart all the way through and
I am the luckiest guy in the world.*

A week later, Helen wrote of her day:

*It's just the prettiest morning. Wish you could come home
for the day, so we could have a picnic. Barbecued chicken or
something real good. Remember?*

*Last night, Mrs. Wood gave me the prettiest gardenia with
a nice long stem. She told me to sleep with it on the pillow
next to me. Imagine such a thing. My sweetheart is much,
much sweeter than that, and they can't fool me with gardenias.
I am smarter than that.*

They eagerly anticipated seeing each other, attempting to coordinate where they would meet — in Columbia or in Salisbury. They pinched pennies to pay for train and bus rides, or to reserve a hotel room in Columbia.

Helen sent Bible verses and detailed notes of Woodbridge's sermons and teachings at First Presbyterian Church. She wrote: "He is such a wonderful man, Darling, and there's no way to ever repay the Lord for sending us to him as he has definitely led both of us to the Lord."

Though they both wrote each other frequently, little was said about the reason Teen was away from home. The war was still distant, even though he was preparing for battle. He was taught how to dig a foxhole and fire a variety of weapons, including an automatic rifle, a machine gun, and a mortar. There were occasions, though, when it crept into Teen's letters.

On March 30, he dropped into the Service Club with pen and paper.

Dearest Sweetheart,

I am really looking forward to the coming weekend in a big way cause it means that we will be together again.

Those moments mean everything to me and I will certainly be glad when this war is over so I can come home to stay. I predict that we will never see actual enemy action as I really feel this war will be over in 12 months. I don't know where I get the idea from, I just feel it in my bones.

They wished each other a million hugs and a million squeezes and a million kisses and heaps of love. Helen frequently referred to Teen as "You sweet ole Booger" and "My Teenie Palm." They spoke of the future when they would set up housekeeping and of the day when a Teenie Junior would be toddling around the house. And always, always, they thanked God for bringing them together and for being an enormous influence in their lives.

In late April, Teen wrote:

Dearest Sweetheart:

Came off of guard a little while ago and just finished making my bed. Got all my clothes unpacked again and once again settled. I am real happy, darling, cause your letter was so sweet. It was waiting for me when I came from guard. I am tired but certainly enjoyed the new experience a great deal. I thought of you all night while I was walking under the stars and looking up at Jesus. The night was beautiful and made me so happy as I walked along praying to Jesus about you and us and thanking him for so much that he has done for us.

In Salisbury, a different form of guard duty had begun: blackouts. Helen was pleased to tell Teen her solution to the mandated darkening of homes and businesses and all city street lights:

Darling, we are to have our first blackout tonight between nine and eleven. I am all ready for bed—in my pajamas, my hair pinned and everything. So when the time comes, I am going to bed. Isn't that a good idea?
I won't cause any trouble.

The blackouts were but one of the many changes taking place on what President Roosevelt called the "Home Front." In Salisbury and across the nation, citizens were advised in posters, newspapers, and radio announcements on how to

"Keep America Free." Residents were urged to spend up to 10 percent of their salaries to buy war bonds. Women joined the workforce in droves to take over jobs vacated by men who had entered the military. Rationing was instituted for a variety of items, including sugar, meat, tires, and gasoline.

Scrap metal collections became regular affairs, and the First Presbyterian Church in Salisbury dismantled a metal fence surrounding the building to contribute to the cause. Americans were pushed to recycle: "Get some cash for your trash." Lumber, paper, kitchen fats, and other items that would formerly have gone to the city dump were being used for production of war supplies. Some people volunteered to be plane-spotters; others became blackout compliance monitors. Fears of invasion by the Japanese or Germans rippled through the country.

Before summer began, both Teen and his brother, Cliff, were sent to Officer Candidate School — Cliff to the Navy, commissioned as an ensign and assigned to the *Jenks*, a destroyer escort that initially served in the Atlantic corridor, protecting ships carrying men and supplies to Europe. He would be aboard the *Jenks* in 1944 when it was part of the naval convoy that captured the German submarine U-505 and its codebooks, enabling the Allies to more precisely locate the deadly U-boats.

Teen was sent to Officer Candidate School at Fort Benning, Georgia, where he was put through several weeks of grueling courses that included artillery, hand-to-hand and house-to-house combat, map reading, and the techniques of infiltration. He worried that he would not be good enough to pass his exams or serve as an officer, but Helen was unfailing in boosting his confidence and reminding him to trust in the Lord.

And Teen was more than thankful for her advice, counsel, and love:

Dearest Sweetheart,

We didn't have such a tough day today as a good part of it was spent in listening to lectures. It's a good thing too, as everyone was a little stiff and sore from the range the day before. The major raised Cain about our range shooting because there were so many men who didn't even qualify and very few sharp-shooters and experts. He said they were going to start clamping the lid down and start getting tougher which I can't see how it would be possible.

I am thankful that Jesus let me get a better score than just qualifying as I know that helps a lot. We will all be in charge of a group of men when we graduate and if we can't do it ourselves, how in the world can we expect to teach or show our men? I couldn't have made it without Jesus.

Some of the boys remark about me saying my prayers or reading my Bible at night. They say they used to do it a long time ago and wish they felt like it now. Only two fellows have called me reverend and chaplain but they have done it only once and I don't think they were kidding as they didn't say it anymore.

It would be wonderful to find a bunch of Christian officers out here. Just look at the men they will be over and what wonderful work they could do for the Lord. I sure do wish for a ten day furlough so I could see you, darling.

I miss you a whole heap and love you more each day. You really are the most wonderful wife in the whole world and I love you to pieces. I wouldn't know where to turn without you, darling.

Graduation from Officer Candidate School was set for early September, and Teen and Helen began planning for the occasion. Teen reserved a hotel room, and Helen arranged her work schedule to take the train. In their daily letters, they counted down the days — not just because it was an important day for Teen, but because it would mean that wherever Teen was sent, they could live together again. They spoke with increasing intensity of their desire to be together, no longer separated by hundreds of miles:

Dearest Sweetheart,

I will be so glad when Sept. 4th comes around as I found out from the boys that it is supposed to be graduation day. I pray real hard each night that I will graduate and be sent somewhere like Washington for the duration so we can live in wonderful happiness and still be close enough to Mount Vernon and Faith so we can visit our folks. I miss you so much, darling, and want this war to be over right away cause I just can't stand living away from you day after day. I want to come home right now.

Love and kisses

Teen was commissioned as a second lieutenant and sent to Camp Wheeler, outside of Macon, Georgia, to be a platoon leader. To their delight, Helen joined him there, and they could live together once more — though usually only on weekends as Teen was often out in the woods and swamps directing maneuvers.

As he prepared to begin training men, he wrote a letter to his mother about his inner turmoil:

Dearest Mother:

You know how I've been about being forward in my life and that most of the time I waited until I was sure before I took on a lot of responsibility. I never was too much on taking the bull by the horns so I guess I'll never grow up from that angle.

I am not afraid to go into combat or afraid of getting hurt — it's leading men into combat that scares me to death because I am responsible for them and I do not know much at all in the field, so naturally I know I am not capable to handle such a gigantic undertaking.

I really didn't think I would be in a situation like I am or I certainly would have waited a lot longer until I got some field experience. I didn't have that training at Benning because they do not have time for drill and basic field principles. I am in a spot where I am trying to teach some things I don't know myself and also learn a million duties besides.

Naturally, I am going to do my best and have no other alternative but to try to do the job.

It's all been a tough fight and still is as I am working night and day. I have faith and know whatever happens it was the Lord's will.

All my love and kisses

As if he could read Teen's mind, his uncle, Lieutenant Colonel Fred Sherrill, a West Point graduate assigned to the U.S. Army Office of the Chief of Engineers in Washington, D.C., wrote to Teen that fall. Though the letter was typewritten and stiff, it was loaded with words of counsel that would resonate powerfully months later when Teen faced the most trying of moments in combat. Sherrill was proud of his nephew, but also understood better than Teen the importance of the duties placed in his young and inexperienced hands:

Dear Teen:

I want to congratulate you on securing a commission in the Army of the United States. You went after the thing the right way and the hard way. Your success in obtaining the commission was a credit to you and to your parents.

If you have not already learned, and I expect you have because you are smart and conscientious, your period of schooling has just begun. A proper handling of men in campaign demands fundamentally that the officers in command have a realization of their responsibility. First of all, to do what they are instructed to do; and second, to do it with the expenditure of as few lives as possible. It is a terrific responsibility. People with a conscience realize it and worry over it.

It should be kept in mind, also, that from the highest ranking General to the lowest ranking Lieutenant, there is no one who knows all the answers or exactly what to do.

We frequently fall into the error of calling War a science. It is at best an art, a risky art, and an art wherein the errors are more frequent than the doing of the right thing. Many a battle, many a campaign, and many a War have been decided not in favor of the side that makes no mistakes, but in favor of the side that makes the fewest costly errors ... You will be confronted with constant changes, confusions, and contradictions. It is these that help make War the miserable mess that it is. Many a man has appeared brilliant when he isn't brilliant — his opponent was dumb. Keep trying to learn, keep a stout heart, and remember that you are in the War for one purpose only — to help to win it just as quickly as possible.

For the next twenty months, Teen worked hard, training soldiers at Camp Wheeler in Georgia, then back at Fort Jackson, South Carolina, where he had started as a private in February 1942, a time that already seemed so long ago. Teen and Helen moved into a room in a dormitory at Columbia Bible College in nearby Columbia. Even when he was miles away on overnight maneuvers, Teen took time to write, and Helen wrote right back. Her letters were encouraging, morale building, and always — always — filled with her expressions of love for Teen and a deep faith and trust in God's plan for their lives.

In early 1944, Teen and his men were sent to the mountains of Tennessee for rigorous training in that terrain. He also had a brief stint at Camp Atterbury, in Edinburgh, Indiana, and then, in April 1944 came the order to report to Fort Meade, a massive infantry training center near Baltimore.

Teen Palm was going overseas.

Helen rode a bus from Salisbury to Fort Meade to meet him. About 4:00 p.m. on April 29, they met in a Service Club on the base to say good-bye. Their parting was not unique. Elsewhere that day and in the hundreds of days before and in many days after, spouses and sweethearts held hands, kissed, made love, and promised they would see each other again. For many, these were, indeed, their last moments together.

Helen kept her chin up, taking some comfort in Teen's assignment to oversee two hundred soldiers on the trip across the Atlantic. She hoped that the responsibility would keep him so busy that he wouldn't have time to get seasick or homesick during the crossing. She could not tell him that she feared she might never see him again.

As they left the club, they embraced and kissed, then squeezed each other tightly.

"I'll be back," Teen whispered. "I know I will."

Her brown curls buried in Teen's neck, Helen squeezed harder, if only to keep back the tears she desperately did not want him to see. She turned and walked away, heading to her hotel room. She would not turn back to show him her tears. Teen turned and walked to his barracks.

Early that evening, though, Helen became restless and even though Teen and all the other soldiers were confined to their barracks, she began to walk toward his unit, hoping only for one last glimpse. When she approached his street, she was confronted by a colonel who looked her straight in the eye, stopping her in her tracks. He opened his mouth as if to reprimand her for being somewhere she was not supposed to be, but when he spoke, his voice was soft.

"Are you looking for someone, Miss?" he asked.

"Yes, I am," Helen replied. "I am looking for Lieutenant Palm."

The colonel looked at her, his eyes softening. "Hey there, lieutenant," the colonel called to a man walking past. "I want you to find Lieutenant Palm and send him here and tell him that he's not to come back to his unit until 10:30."

In what seemed like hours to Helen but was only a matter of seconds, Teen strolled up the street, grinning broadly. They embraced and then, arm in arm, began walking.

Helen recounted the evening in a letter she wrote the following day to Teen's mother in Mount Vernon:

Dear Mother,

Last night my sweetheart left. His leaving almost tore my heart right out — yet for his sake, I was pretty well-behaved.

We spent our last hour sitting on a little bench near a bus

*stop and in that one hour, I realized all over again how good
the Lord had been back there on June 7, 1941 to unite us as
man and wife. Seeing him go was one of the hardest things I
have had to endure. But we stand on the promise of God—
"All things work together for good to them that love God."*

Shortly after midnight, less than two hours after they
parted for the second time, Teen was gone. Days later, he sat
down aboard ship and composed a letter to his mother:

Dearest Mother,

*Our trip is three-fourths over and in a few more days, we
should land again ... I never realized it took such a long time
to cross a body of water and I have never been so tired of
looking at nothing but water.*

*We are looking to the future and wondering just what is in
store for us all. We are all agreeable on one thing and that is
this—There is no place like home in the good old USA and if
we get back sooner than expected, we hope to travel no more
again. I know one thing—when I get back to Helen, I'll never
let her out of my sight again. I wish we had a family as I am
not getting any younger and it may be a while before I get
back.*

All my love

Within days, he arrived in England, joining thousands of
other soldiers, all of them wondering when they would cross
the English Channel and plunge into battle. He was tough and
ready for combat. When drafted little more than two years
earlier, Teen weighed two hundred pounds. Now, he was two
hundred pounds of muscle and grit.

CHAPTER 8

AT THE CASABLANCA CONFERENCE OF JANUARY 14–24, 1943, while Palm was preparing his men for war, Roosevelt and Churchill agreed to seek the "unconditional surrender" of the Axis powers and nothing less. They laid plans for the invasion of Italy and Sicily. That summer, the British chiefs of staff received details for Operation Overlord, the code name for the fifty-mile-long invasion of northwestern France across the English Channel.

Near the end of the year, General Dwight D. Eisenhower assumed the post of Supreme Commander Allied Expeditionary Force and a month later American soldiers and sailors began practicing landings along the shores of Chesapeake Bay. Endless convoys of ships transporting troops, tanks, artillery, munitions, trucks, and other weapons of war continued to make their way to England. Troops practiced landings on the British coast, and U.S. Rangers repeatedly scaled cliffs along the coast as well as inland.

Beginning in 1940, Radio London, broadcasting from a studio at the British Broadcasting Corporation, sent numerous messages from Free French Forces to the French Resistance in France. In early June 1944, many messages broadcast were meaningless, but some were not. On June 1 and June 5, an announcer said, *"Blessent mon cœur d'une langeur monotone."* The phrase, translated as "Wound my heart with a monotonous languor," came from Paul Verlaine's poem "The Song of Autumn" and signaled that the Allies were preparing to attack.

At 9:15 p.m. on June 5, 1944, Radio London aired several more messages that, to the casual listener, seemed nonsensical: "The carrots are cooked. The dice have been thrown."

But to resistance forces, these were exciting words because they signaled an invasion of France. The following day, June 6 — D-Day — Eisenhower sent a message to the troops:

Soldiers, Sailors and Airmen of the Allied Expeditionary Force! You are about to embark upon the Great Crusade, toward which we have striven these many months. The eyes of the world are upon you. The hopes and prayers of liberty-loving people everywhere march with you. In company with our brave Allies and brothers-in-arms on other fronts, you will bring about the destruction of the German war machine, the elimination of Nazi tyranny over the oppressed peoples of Europe, and security for ourselves in a free world. Your task will not be an easy one. Your enemy is well trained, well-equipped and battle-hardened. He will fight savagely.

But this is the year 1944! Much has happened since the Nazi triumphs of 1940 – 41. The United Nations have inflicted upon the Germans great defeats, in open battle, man-to-man. Our air offensive has seriously reduced their strength in the air and their capacity to wage war on the ground. Our home fronts have given us an overwhelming superiority in weapons and munitions of war, and placed at our disposal great reserves of trained fighting men. The tide has turned! The free men of the world are marching together to Victory!

I have full confidence in your courage and devotion to duty and skill in battle. We will accept nothing less than full Victory! Good luck! And let us beseech the blessing of Almighty God upon this great and noble undertaking.

On the evening of June 5, under the protection of eleven thousand Allied bombers and fighter planes, more than five thousand vessels began plowing toward the French coast and Hitler's Atlantic Wall, a system of coastal fortifications that stretched from the Pyrenees north across the length of Norway.

Shortly before midnight, more than eight hundred C-47 transport planes, some carrying American, British, and Canadian paratroopers, and some towing gliders filled with assault troops, began to fill the skies over the English Channel. Over French soil, paratroopers by the thousands began the perilous descent. Many were killed in the sky and floated lifelessly to the ground. Others died in firefights almost immediately after landing. Some assault soldiers were killed when their gliders crashed. Still, a significant number of men survived.

While Teen waited in England, the invasion began in the predawn darkness. At 5:30 a.m., battleships began a ferocious shelling of the French coast. From 6:30 to 7:55 a.m., thousands of men climbed down rope ladders hanging on the sides of transport ships miles off the coast. They clambered into landing crafts to begin the journey toward land. The winds and waves were much more powerful than expected. Some crafts foundered in the roiling sea. Others were blown apart by German artillery or struck undersea obstacles and sank. Some managed to get through unscathed, but when their front doors were lowered, the first rows of soldiers who charged were slaughtered by machine-gun fire. Some soldiers, over-weighted by their equipment, drowned when they stepped into water over their heads. On the beach, soldiers faced artillery and mortar blasts. Some men confronted the extremely difficult task of scaling sheer cliffs towering one hundred to one hundred fifty feet above them.

The cost was high — of the more than one hundred fifty-six thousand men deployed on D-Day, some nine to ten thousand were killed, wounded, or missing in action. The following morning, June 7, the largest flotilla of ships in history filled the horizon off the beaches of the Normandy coast, awaiting their turn to deposit thousands more men and tons of guns and supplies on that newly acquired sliver of land.

That the nearly thirty-five thousand men of the 1st and 29th U.S. Infantry Divisions had established a beachhead at Omaha Beach seemed nothing less than a miracle. The seasoned German 352nd Infantry Division, manning carefully engineered fortifications and tunnels, outnumbered the initial American assault waves by a ratio of four to three. German guns at the tops of bluffs had been fortified so that the weapons suffered relatively little damage in the furious aerial and naval bombardments that preceded the invasion. German artillery and machine guns raked the beaches in a murderous crossfire. Several hundred yards inland from the ocean's waterline ran a fifteen-foot-deep ditch packed with landmines and covered with a thicket of barbed-wire entrapments. Soldiers who survived the crossing of the beach to reach the ditch were exposed to continuous machine-gun fire.

Underneath the waters off-shore, six-pronged "spiders," made of crossed iron railroad rails and ties, along with large sharpened logs, ripped open and impaled the hulls of landing craft. Some of the spiders protruded high over the water line. Czech Hedgehogs (three metal girders or sections of rail welded together at the middle) blocked entrance to the shore. Floating mines tore apart landing craft and soldiers alike in sudden fiery blasts. Strong currents pulled some landing crafts away from their assigned destinations.

For five miles along the crescent shoreline of Omaha Beach, bodies were strewn among the wreckage of half tracks, flipped landing crafts, blasted tanks, crippled bulldozers, tangled barbed wire and telephone lines. Underneath the sea, extending for a mile and beyond from the shore, lay sunken landing crafts — some with their soldiers silently entombed within them — as well as boats bearing tanks and trucks and their crews.

Strewn across the sand was the detritus of soldiers' packs: diaries, Bibles, snapshots of loved ones, cherished letters from home, toothbrushes, and lifebelts. Fallen soldiers lay crumpled on the beach as if sleeping. Bodies of those who died in the water rolled limply toward shore in the tide and then were drawn back into the ocean. Soldiers assigned to collect the dead lined the bodies in rows and draped them with covers so that only their boots were visible.

The assault on Omaha Beach constituted only one element of Operation Overlord. Some one hundred fifty-six thousand troops participated in the invasion, seventy-three thousand in the American sector of Utah Beach and Omaha Beach, and eighty-three thousand in the British and Canadian sector of Gold Beach, Juno Beach, and Sword Beach. Other nations — Czechoslovakia, France, Greece, Holland, New Zealand, Norway, and Poland — also contributed troops to the invasion forces.

As night fell in America on D-Day, President Roosevelt

delivered a radio message, asking the nation to join him in prayer:

Our sons, pride of our nation, this day have set upon a mighty endeavor, a struggle to preserve our Republic, our religion, and our civilization, and to set free a suffering humanity. Lead them straight and true; give strength to their arms, stoutness to their hearts, steadfastness in their faith.

They will need Thy blessings. Their road will be long and hard. For the enemy is strong. He may hurl back our forces. Success may not come with rushing speed, but we shall return again and again; and we know that by Thy grace, and by the righteousness of our cause, our sons will triumph.

They will be sore tried, by night and by day, without rest — until the victory is won. The darkness will be rent by noise and flame. Men's souls will be shaken with the violences of war. For these men are lately drawn from the ways of peace. They fight not for the lust of conquest. They fight to end conquest. They fight to liberate. They fight to let justice arise, and tolerance and goodwill among all Thy people.

That night, as he did every night, Teen, who was waiting in England to be deployed in the D-Day follow-up waves, composed a letter to Helen:

Dearest Sweetheart:

Well, it finally happened and I know the eyes of the world are focused on us over here. I guess this day will be a big memory in all our lives as it means the beginning of the end for Hitler.

I am still shivering, though, as the weather is cold. We all could get along a lot nicer if we had a little stove in here. I guess I am selfish as there are a lot of boys on the beach head tonight in the invasion that would think this little tent was a cozy home. We all had a service and prayed for all of them that this war may end soon and that the suffering would not be too great out there.

Once the Normandy coast was secured, reinforcement troops accompanied by huge amounts of war equipment landed on Allied beachheads and began fighting their way into the interior of France.

By June 13, a third wave of Allied forces had hit the beaches of France, bringing Allied troop strength to more than three hundred and fifty thousand. Teen wrote a letter to his sister, Gladys, telling her that he was ready to go into battle. He made no reference to the horrible casualties inflicted during the D-Day invasion:

Dear Glad:

I am still located in the same place and have nothing but favorable reports to give. The boys in France are doing a swell job and we are right behind them waiting to go in and do our share. We have been playing a lot of chess with the officers here. I'm still the champ, but don't know how long it will last.

We played the officers from another company last night in touch football but got trounced 30 – 0. Still cold and rainy here and still stays light until 11:30 pm.

Love and kisses

By mid-July, following fierce fighting, U.S. troops had taken control of Saint-Lo, a key crossroad city in Normandy. British and Canadian troops were pushing toward Caen, which was forty miles to the east. But the forces were battling to break out of Normandy.

By then, some of the troops involved in the D-Day invasion were being sent back to England. Their descriptions of the carnage and of their survival instilled an even greater urgency among those still waiting for assignment. They wanted to shoulder their share of the burden.

Teen was moved by the stories he heard, as he related in a letter to his mother:

Dearest Mother:

I have talked to a lot of men who were in the invasion and it really gives you a new slant on things. I hope to be able to get in a combat outfit soon so I can get to the front and do my share.

An officer in my tent has been alerted and is packing to go to France. I guess when the day comes for me to go, I will be sending a lot of stuff home. I believe in traveling light as I want to have most of my load consisting of firearms, knife and ammunition with a few pockets left for my C rations. I am getting anxious to get up there. I hate to come this far with all my training not to get into the fight.

Teen was anxious, his nights filled with dreams of battle. He described one to Helen, a particularly vivid and disturbing dream he had about a high school classmate who had been sent to fight in North Africa. Teen was concerned that his dream meant that his friend was killed:

It seems that we were in a school room again and he had on his uniform with a lot of ribbons including a Purple Heart. In our dream we embraced each other and talked about combat. It gave me a funny feeling as I have written to him without ever getting a reply. Ever since that dream, I have been wanting to go into a combat outfit up in France as I feel it is the real place for me right now. I know the Lord will take care of me up there under fire and I am not afraid of anything. I just feel that I am not doing my part by staying in England when all the boys need all the help they can get up there in the line. I feel like I am wearing lace on my breeches instead of wearing my combat uniform with boots, pistol belt and carbine rifle.

Teen was working as a special services officer, organizing mail call, overseeing mess hall, and arranging for entertainment for the troops. He supervised construction of an amphitheater with electricity to show movies and one evening got a glimpse of war up close. "We had a film showing all the war pictures on the invasion of France," he wrote Helen. "I don't see how the photographers were able to get in so close without getting the camera blown to bits. Some of them did get killed."

Though Hitler had ordered that Paris "must not fall into the enemy's hand except lying in complete debris" and that it was to be leveled by bombing, the German surrender of the French capital to Allied forces took place without such devastation on August 25, 1944. Deliriously happy crowds welcomed Charles de Gaulle into Paris as remaining German snipers were systematically tracked down and suppressed. Teen wrote to Helen, saying he was hopeful he would be able to go home soon:

*I am really looking west toward home and hope one of these
months to take that return trip.*

*If you can, listen to Frank Sinatra's recording of "My
Shining Hour." It's beautiful and I think of you every time I
play it. It reminds me of you, darling, and how I dream of you
all the time. Listen to it if you can as I dedicate it to you as a
sequel to our other song, "I'll Get By," for when I get home we
will take our usual evening rides again and I'll sing it for you.*

Home had to wait. In September, Teen crossed the English Channel in a landing craft and waded ashore on Omaha
Beach. He was astonished by the devastation: the shattered
fortifications and wrecked pill boxes, craters made by artillery shells, and foxholes built for protection.

The men pitched their tents and awaited orders. They lived
on C rations with three variations of the main course — meat
and beans, meat and potato hash, or meat and vegetable — as
well as four hardtack biscuits and three gum drops. They took
cold-water sponge baths. They bartered with French citizens
for bread and eggs.

As he marched through the French towns of Vire, Flers,
Argentan, and Alençon, and headed toward Paris, he was
awed by the destruction. He wrote Helen:

*The towns are all in rubble with few houses left standing.
The people are worse off than the British and this makes all
the British ruins look like child's play. I have seen people
returning to their ruined towns with all of their possessions
piled on the horse-drawn two-wheeled carts.*

*Along the roads, I have seen crashed Nazi planes, and
tanks and armored cars blown up or burned out. I have seen
some of ours, too. I saw a lot of graves in twos and fours and*

sixes. I mean our boys. They were buried near the French
farmhouses where they fell with crosses made of wood and
their helmets on the head of the grave. I have seen enough
now to make this war real to me and close at hand. I don't
mind doing the things I have to do like bathing in streams and
living in my pup tent as there are boys up front who can't even
do these things.

One of his first encounters with the enemy came one morning when, as he related to Helen:

We had a German about sixteen years of age give himself
up to us. He had been hiding out in the woods hoping for a
counterattack that never came. He looked very weak and
said he had not eaten for four days. He wanted us to take him
prisoner, which, of course, we did.
*   War is such a folly when you see things like that. But the*
German people must be taught a lesson this time that they
never will forget. I hope we can do that job within the next
year.

CHAPTER 9

TEEN PALM, A MEMBER OF THE 106TH INFANTRY DIVISION, was transferred to the 45th Infantry Division, a storied group that traced its roots back to the formation of the Militia of the Territory in Oklahoma in 1890. The unit's original insignia was a swastika, a common Native American symbol, in deference to the many Native Americans who made up the unit. But with the rise of the Nazi Party, the shoulder sleeve patch was changed to a Thunderbird, a mythological creature capable of bringing rain and creating thunder by beating its wings.

After the Thunderbird Division was activated for the war in 1940, it was organized into three infantry regiments, four field artillery battalions, a signal company, an ordinance company, a quartermaster company, a reconnaissance company, an engineer battalion, and a medical battalion.

Each infantry regiment was composed of about three thousand men, and within each regiment were numerous companies, each having anywhere from 60 to 190 soldiers and designated by a letter of the alphabet and referred to using words that began with those letters. For example, Company A was Able Company, Company B was Baker, C was Charlie, and so on. Within each company were platoons made up of as few as sixteen soldiers and as many as sixty.

Palm was assigned to Company B of the 179th Infantry. He was to oversee a platoon at the frontline in mid-October. The men of the 179th had been fighting continuously and furiously since mid-August. They engaged in deadly assaults and had been at times forced to fall back. Their ranks were depleted — some taken prisoner, numerous others killed or wounded. More ominous for Palm, the life expectancy of a lieutenant on the front lines during that time was less than three weeks.

Sergeant Stan Swinton, a writer for the overseas edition of *Stars and Stripes*, the newspaper that served the armed forces, described the battle for the town of Grandvilliers in northern France:

> The battle began on the morning of Sept. 30 when Company B of the 179th Infantry Regiment ... advanced with the support of a platoon of light tanks. Not until the doughboys had penetrated almost to the center of Grandvilliers did serious opposition develop. Then a hail of small arm and mortar fire pinned them down ... An antitank gun and mines forced the armor to withdraw. The infantry dug in beside the ancient church whose narrow, conical spire juts upward from its sloping red-tiled roof to dominate the village. There ... under fire that did not slacken until 3 a.m., Baker Company stayed.

Swinton's narrative told how on the following afternoon, Company B shoved off again, gained three hundred yards, but was halted again. A group of nine soldiers took cover behind a stone wall and traded fire until 8:30 p.m. with German soldiers in a house twenty feet away. Then quiet fell until the Germans shouted for the nine men to surrender. The response was a barrage of American bullets. The Germans answered by charging on foot, stepping over their fallen comrades.

Until 2:00 a.m., the Germans kept coming, Swinton reported. The attack was finally halted when the Americans, their ammunition almost depleted, began lobbing hand grenades. By then, tanks had come up to support Company B, and two other companies had pushed the Germans out of the woods surrounding the town.

On October 2, tanks began a house-by-house assault, followed by six-man squads of infantrymen, killing or capturing German soldiers in each house. Swinton reported:

> By nightfall the battle was almost over. A single pocket between Baker and Charlie Companies was cleaned out at 1 a.m. to end the fighting. Now the tired, bearded doughboys have pushed a few [hundred] yards further. Grandvillers is behind them.

This took place ten days before Palm arrived at the front. And when he did, he found himself on the move, slogging and crawling along knolls and ridges, through thickets and woods. At night, sitting in his foxhole covered with logs, chilled by the autumn rain, he scribbled letters to Helen that would be dispatched in the Army mail when conditions allowed. His first letter only hinted at the terror of battle after he had experienced raw combat:

> *It's been a week since I have written because I am now on the front lines. This has been my first week of combat and the Lord has certainly been with us through it all. It hasn't been as bad as it could have been, only the shelling makes you sweat in a hole while it is dropping around you. We have had some pretty good success and the company has had our share of capturing prisoners. The fighting is terrific due to the dense woods and sometimes you can throw rocks on the Jerries.*

*I went on a recon patrol with my platoon sergeant and
I almost stepped on two Krauts lying in the bushes, so you
can see how it is. The boys' morale is good, considering what
living at the front is like.*

*It's a funny feeling when you go up a hill in an attack,
knowing that there is something there that will shoot back at
you. You are scared, sure, but somehow your job keeps you
going. I have a good platoon and they really stick together.*

*Here at the front, we just live from day to day. Right now,
we are having a day's rest just back of the lines and I finally
got a chance to tell you I am OK.*

Days later, he was back at the front as the 179th continued
its march to the Rhine River. He wrote to Helen:

*The weather is terrible — raining and cold. This whole
business is like an ugly nightmare and I want to wake up
quickly to find you with me again with us both back home.*

*These Krauts keep fighting on and on even though they
know it's a losing battle. We gave them a good pasting the last
three weeks and pushed them back a few more miles, but we
also had to lick a few of our wounds in doing so. I can't say
much about our activities and it's just as well as I don't want
to worry you with the war business.*

*Pray real hard for us all, darling. Have everyone else pray
for us as I know it's the only way this war will stop. It sure is
amazing how you can appreciate the bare necessities of life
by just being alive. These medals we are piling up by being
in combat mean nothing to me now. All I want to do is come
home. I have seen enough of combat to satisfy me the rest of
my days.*

What he had seen, Palm would soon discover, was only the

beginning. On a good day, he was able to sleep in a home and stay out of the elements. On other days, he was in a foxhole. The men often slept two to a foxhole in order to curl up next to each other for warmth.

Foxholes were their best and often only protection. Each time the troops halted, the men pulled out axes, spades, and tree saws and began working furiously. Men with shovels dug pits about seven to eight feet long, four feet wide, and three feet deep. Men with saws cut down small trees into five-foot lengths, which were laid across the pits, leaving an opening at one end. Men with shovels then covered the logs with dirt from the holes. These foxholes protected them from artillery and mortar shells, as well as the splintered tree branches and tree trunks that became projectiles when hit by the shells.

In early November, Teen was part of a group of men who were sent to the rear of the front lines for a rest after twenty-one consecutive days of combat. He wrote a letter to his sister, Gladys, describing some of his experiences.

Dearest Glad,

The weather is rough and it is snowing outside. I really feel for the boys on the front lines and I know what they are suffering. I certainly had some experiences in the past three weeks that I will long remember the rest of my days. Of course I expect to be back at the front in another two weeks after this rest is over and I don't mind admitting that it makes me sweat to think about what might be in the future for me.

It is a funny feeling when you advance forward with your men not knowing what is on that slope or hill or in that draw. I have been on some hair-raising patrols and would like to tell you about some battles I have been in and what happened but that is not to be told till after the war.

The Jerries are just as scared in battle as can be—we are too, for that matter—the first machine gun that opened fire on me made my toe nails curl up but thanks to the Lord I was not hit. Some of the things are funny to think over and I get some laughs but a lot of incidents are not so funny and sometimes have their sad notes.

I have a real good platoon of men and I am proud of them for what they have done and how they have carried on. I still have a lot to learn and hope for greater courage in my next campaign. We were on the edge of a small town and were going to go in and take it but ran into too much fire and too many Jerries.

The ground was too open to expose our men and I had to go down to the edge of a woods with a map of the town to get a good view of the open terrain and made a report to the C.O. I don't mind saying that as I made my way down on the mission knowing Jerry was out there pretty thick, you could have played a tune on me with a violin bow, my muscles and nerves were so tense and tight.

Something inside tells you not to take the chance but the call of duty and something else keeps you going.

My platoon sergeant and I usually dig in and sleep together when we are on the line. He is quite a comical guy and a long lanky Texan about 37 years old. I have a lot of confidence in him as he is a veteran where combat is concerned. His name is Simpson, but we call him Slim for short.

The mud in France is still terrific and tough to go through. You can see that in the papers, though, and realize that it slows down operations. I am part of the Seventh Army, so you can keep track of me in the papers when you read about the Seventh.

When his leave was over, Palm returned to the front. He

was there in time to spend Thanksgiving eve in a Catholic church and ate Thanksgiving dinner out of his mess kit before shoving off in the early morning hours. He and his men slashed forward, wiping out pockets of German soldiers as they moved into a forest northwest of Engwiller. There they were stopped by a ferocious assault from German tanks. Under the cover of a smoke screen launched by a barrage of mortar and artillery fire, American tanks sped forward. The ensuing battle lasted much of the day. The Germans finally ceded the town, but not before Palm faced a day of death and courage.

On December 1, a patrol had returned to Company B to report a heavy concentration of German troops just outside a small nearby town. The company commander, Lieutenant John Rahill, organized a group of men that included Palm to go after the Germans.

Though he was only twenty years old, Rahill was already a combat veteran. A native of New Jersey, he had hitchhiked across the country by the time he was seventeen, and when the war came, he dropped out of the University of Chicago and enlisted. His first taste of battle came in January 1944 when he had come ashore with the 179th at Anzio in southern Italy. He fought northward in the Allied invasion of southern France, earning a Silver Star for heroism when he came under fire from a rapidly approaching tank. He radioed in for American artillery to launch shells virtually on his own position. The tank was destroyed and Rahill narrowly survived.

Rahill and Palm had more than their uniforms and weapons in common. Both carried Bibles into combat, and both frequently wrote home about how they were trusting in God as they ducked and dodged bullets and artillery shells.

After the war, Lieutenant Robert M. Barnhart, who like

Palm commanded a platoon in Company B, recalled that Rahill had a maturity far beyond his years. Barnhart said that Rahill frequently advised his men: "Don't agonize by thinking of how things used to be and wishing you had these things now. The reality is, what you are doing right now is your life. Take pleasure in anything you can, but don't ponder on the past."

Palm and Rahill and several other men headed toward the German forces, working their way through a densely wooded area. As they reached the edge of the forest, they were confronted by an open field. A church steeple was visible in the distance over the tops of trees at the end of the field.

Cautiously, the men maneuvered out of the woods and up to the side of a road. They barely got twenty yards before the Germans, likely alerted by a scout positioned in the church steeple, launched a ferocious barrage of mortar, artillery, tank, and small-arms fire.

"Get off the road! Get in the ditch!" Rahill yelled.

In a memoir later, Barnhart recalled that on that day he was at the company command post, being held in reserve to monitor signals from Rahill's radio. "Suddenly we heard a tremendous barrage. One explosion was so loud that I thought it might break the speaker on our radio. Then we heard the radio man say, 'Lieutenant Rahill is dead.' "

After one hundred consecutive days of fighting on the front line without a scratch, Rahill was within a few feet of a mortar round. A piece of shrapnel struck his shirt pocket, punctured a hole in the photograph of his fiancée, and pierced his heart. Another fragment pierced his thigh and severed his femoral artery. He bled to death in minutes.

Several other men were downed, though still alive. James O'Donnell had seventy two shrapnel wounds. O'Donnell later recalled that Rahill's command to take cover were his last words.

With Rahill dead and others wounded, Company B was in chaos. The men were scattered and disorganized, hugging the ground, seeking any kind of shelter in the hope of staying alive.

Palm immediately took command of the company and, in the face of the thunderous fusillade, began shouting. "Regroup! Stand your ground! Stick together!"

Quickly, he moved from man to man, exposing himself to enemy fire, exhorting, urging them to keep fighting. And gradually, the men moved forward and knocked out the enemy force.

For his gallantry that day, Palm was later awarded a Silver Star, one of the highest military awards. The citation would read: "Lieutenant Palm assumed command and by moving among the men, encouraging them and directing their deployment, reorganized the company to continue the attack. With Lieutenant Palm leading it in the face of the heavy enemy fire, the company went on to take its objective."

Two days later, Teen wrote to Helen:

Dearest Sweetheart:

Just a note while passing along the road to tell you that I am getting along fine and am in good health. The Lord is wonderful in all his mercy. I am sure missing you, darling, and want to come home to you in a big way. I know that even though I don't like it and hate this fighting, I am going to have to stick until it's over as you can't quit. I am continually trusting in the Lord for my every need and thanking him every day for you and to bring us together.

All my love and kisses

Not once did he mention the events of the day Rahill fell in battle. His reticence at describing his exploits — whether driven by humility or his concern over alarming Helen or the thought that such detail would be censored — would continue far beyond this letter.

The 179th pushed toward the Rhine River and Germany. On the afternoon of Christmas Eve, Palm and a few other soldiers found themselves in the home of a French family. Though part of the home had been demolished by artillery shells, the family gathered with the soldiers in front of a decorated Christmas tree and they all sang carols — in English and French. They feasted on pies baked with sugar that the family had hoarded for months.

On December 27, Teen warned Helen not to become too optimistic:

> *Don't let the headlines in the paper fool folks back home as they print too rosy a picture. Some days we are lucky to go 500 yards. We have been issued wool fleece-lined coats. It's very cold. I pray for good, clear weather so our Air Force can get out as we really need them to give us support.*

The Allies were advancing gradually, but German counterattacks at times forced retreats, and Allied positions were overrun. On December 19, 1944, two regiments of the 106th Infantry Division, Teen's former division, had suffered a great loss of life and the survivors had been forced to surrender to the Germans.

On January 14, Palm earned another major battle citation, a Bronze Star with Oak Leaf Cluster for his actions during a vicious firefight near Kohlhutte, only miles from the German border. The company commander was wounded, and Palm assumed command of the company and continued moving forward, only to wind up in a heavily mined field.

The explosions when someone triggered a mine were deafening, and men were hurtled through the air in a spray of blood and amid agonized shouts. Some soldiers were frozen on the ground, afraid to move for fear of triggering a mine. Others were scrabbling toward the rear.

Palm, barking orders, reorganized the men and oversaw a safe withdrawal of those who could still move. Within three hours, he selected a small group of men and, under heavy artillery fire, led them back where they evacuated the wounded.

By the end of January, Palm's thirty-second birthday had passed without note. He was spending his days and nights in a command post dug out of the ground and reinforced with logs. Snow continued to fall, rising to knee-depth in places. His unit was standing still for the time being, behind the front line. One afternoon, he and two other officers found time to head into the woods and shoot a deer. That night, in the midst of the death and destruction, soldiers celebrated with charred venison steak.

Still, the pressure and danger and physical strain were telling in his letters:

> I don't feel like pushing anymore. I certainly have had my fill of that and each time you push, it means so many less faces in the outfit.
>
> We had a church service outside of the command post last night and sang softly so the Jerries wouldn't hear us. It's odd to hear a shell go over in the middle of prayer when all is quiet.

In February, Palm was among a number of officers given a three-day pass to Paris. Upon his return, he began several weeks of training and brushing up on marksmanship, map reading, and reconnaissance. He was joined by a new company commander: Captain William Robertson, a rancher from Okmulgee, Oklahoma. Robertson had fought in the 45th Division for two years before being given a leave to return home. But after two months, he was summoned back to the front. Palm revered him. He would later call Robertson the best commander he had ever worked with, particularly in combat.

Robertson was their leader as their training shifted to a new focus: crossing the Rhine River and, at last, putting Germany and Hitler squarely in their gun sights.

CHAPTER 10

THERE COULD BE NO CROSSING OF THE RHINE UNLESS THE Allies could breach Hitler's infamous Siegfried Line, a nearly four-hundred-mile fortification of bunkers, pillboxes, and tank traps, stretching from the Netherlands on the north to Switzerland on the south.

After the D-Day invasion, Hitler ordered the line, also called the Westwall, to be refortified and strengthened, primarily with slave labor. Constructed of concrete and steel, the barrier was formidable. It was protected by minefields and rows of "dragons' teeth," small pyramid-shaped fortifications made of reinforced concrete designed to impede the movement of tanks. Troops who managed to get beyond these defenses faced concrete pillboxes housing machine guns that could sweep vast areas of land.

When the 45th Division began its assault on the line on March 17, the 179th Infantry Regiment was at its center. An account of that day was captured in *Thunderbird: A History of the 45th Infantry Division* by Guy Nelson:

> [The] assault was slow and deadly. Under a protective artillery and tank barrage leveled at gun emplacements, tanks and infantry advanced on the dragon's teeth.

Infantry units blasted openings in the concrete rows and the tanks moved through. The tanks then leveled their firepower at the concrete pillboxes and infantry units moved up to [take them out] one by one.

By day's end, twenty-four pillboxes had been knocked out.

The resulting gaps created openings that the troops capitalized upon the following day. Each regiment methodically blasted its way forward through the line against withering opposition. By the end of the second day, eighty-six more pillboxes had been destroyed and two hundred and sixty-eight German soldiers had been taken prisoner. Despite some occasional counterattacks, the Germans were clearly on the defensive — the backbone of their defenses was shattered.

On March 19, Teen Palm found a moment to write to his mother:

I am battling my way through Germany and doing OK. It's a case of these people getting a dose of their own medicine. The towns we have captured so far have taken a beating and we had to put up a good fight to get in.

On March 20, the German Army abandoned its positions. Throughout the day, the German withdrawal became more and more disorganized. Large columns of troops were captured as the retreat became a rout.

The 45th Division renewed its attack and quickly overtook the Germans, capturing nearly two thousand soldiers who were attempting to flee.

"All three 179th battalions sped after the enemy, taking 451 prisoners of war in the day," wrote Nelson. "They assaulted the city of Homburg, fighting through it street by street and house by house, until finally, in the late hours of the night, all enemy soldiers had been captured or killed."

That night, Palm wrote to friends in Salisbury, asking a favor — to buy Helen "the biggest and nicest orchid in town for Easter."

Now, the 179th headed for Bliesbruck, fifteen miles southwest of Homburg. The only route was across an open field. The soldiers were greeted with heavy bursts from a machine gun in a concrete bunker as well as sniper fire. After several minutes, a soldier crept next to the side of the machine-gun bunker and tossed in a grenade. Then he moved in and gunned down the four German soldiers inside. With the machine gun silenced, Palm's Company B moved into town. For several hours, it moved house to house, killing German soldiers and taking others prisoner until the town was secured.

Teen described the battle in a letter to Helen:

I have been riding on tanks, fighting from town to town in a fast push which has put us a good ways into Germany.

I can tell you our first battle in Germany and the toughest so far was at Bliesbruck. We fought like mad for two days against an SS company and when we finished, the town was leveled by tanks. We left it a ghost town. We finally broke the back of the Siegfried line.

Up next was the Rhine River.

The Allied Command ordered a series of crossings at different locations along the Rhine. In a daring stroke, on March 7, 1945, the 9th Armored Division seized the Remagen Bridge, the only viable standing bridge across the river, and quickly rushed across to establish a beachhead. The 5th Infantry

Division, part of General George S. Patton's Third Army, crossed at Oppenheim on March 22.

The 45th Division was ordered to cross the Rhine on March 26 near Worms, a formidable task because the river at that location was one thousand feet wide and seventeen feet deep.

Captain Robertson summoned Palm and ordered him to organize Company B into boat teams. Palm had to combine some platoons because the battalion had suffered serious casualties during the assault on the Siegfried Line and was depleted. He called the platoon leaders together and handed out boat assignments and maps.

He explained that upon crossing the river, the men would have to traverse a narrow strip of open land before being confronted by a fifty-foot-wide canal. Beyond the canal was a heavy patch of woods. Here, according to aerial reconnaissance, Germans were dug in and had machine guns in positions so they could easily cover all river approaches. The Americans' mission: clear out the Germans from beyond the canal and sweep through the woods.

At 8:00 p.m. on March 25, Company B was loaded onto trucks and driven to the village of Osthofen. From there the men moved on foot to an orchard bordering the river. The crossing was set for 2:30 a.m. Eighteen boats were already in place at the edge of the woods, stashed under trees and camouflage netting.

The moon was obscured by clouds, but there was still enough light for the men to make out forms moving in the darkness. The troops huddled under cover of the orchard. For several hours, they could only wait. They were prohibited from speaking out loud—all commands and instructions had to be whispered—for fear of giving away their location.

As they waited, the men heard the sound of approaching aircraft — German bombers flying so low that the troops could see fire squirting from the exhaust pipes of their gasoline-powered motors. The planes dropped scores of flares, lighting the sky. As the planes flew into the distance, several were hit — it was impossible to tell if they were attacked by other planes or hit by antiaircraft fire. One plane exploded in the air.

Anxiously, the silent soldiers wondered whether the Germans were trying to signal that they knew the river was about to be crossed. Some feared they were headed for a slaughter. One soldier panicked, shot himself in the foot, and was immediately dragged out of the orchard. Every man held his breath, wondering if the gunshot had given away their presence.

Palm stood under an apple tree, going through a mental checklist. Two years earlier, he would have been craving a cigarette, but he had kicked the habit many months before. Many of his men — boys, really — had only taken up the habit since they had arrived at the front. There would be no smoking on this night, however.

Palm was soon joined by Robertson, and both hunkered down to rest and wait.

Robertson had given his orders earlier. "On reaching the shore, the 1st and 2nd Platoons will go to the bank of the canal. The 2nd will make an end run, skirting the canal, on the right to a bridge which spans the canal. They will cross the bridge, move through the woods and set up a line of defense at the woods furthest from the river. The 3rd Platoon will follow and secure the woods facing downstream."

Robertson had then paused.

"There can be no alternate plan," he said. "No withdrawal."

At 2:20 a.m., messengers were sent among the troops, alerting them to start for the boats, which they were to carry fifty yards to the water's edge. As the boats launched, their fifty-five horsepower motors sounding like a million swarming bees, the 157th Infantry Regiment opened up with supporting machine-gun fire that sent thousands of bullets screaming over the heads of the men as they sped toward the far shore. The glare of the gunfire gave the men an eerie glow as they clenched the gunwales of the boats. As they approached, white tracers from German guns pierced the darkness.

Robertson's boat arrived first and idled in the water just short of the river bank so he could fire a flare. This was a signal for the supporting machine gun fire to halt so the soldiers would not wound or kill their comrades. Enemy rifle fire began to erupt from the shore. One American, part of the 2nd Platoon headed for the bridge over the canal, avoided the sudden burst of German machine gun by diving into a ditch. There he landed on top of a German soldier, who promptly surrendered and pointed out the position of the machine gun. Moments later, the gun was silenced by grenades.

Swiftly, hundreds of men hit the banks and moved forward. The assault was so effective that some Germans surrendered while still in their foxholes, as their positions were overrun in the darkness. Two soldiers were assigned to escort seven prisoners to a boat, but as they walked to the shore, they were ambushed by other Germans. Both Americans were shot and killed. Troops sent to the rear recaptured the prisoners and caught the attackers.

Palm moved stealthily and steadily into the woods, firing at anything that moved. Robertson directed the men through the woods and into the nearby town of Gross Rohrheim, which had already been secured by Company A.

Company B lost two men — both killed — but was otherwise intact. The company had killed five Germans and captured twenty-two. By dusk that day, March 26, more than two hundred Germans had been captured.

The advance gained momentum. Town after town began to fall as the 45th Division picked up speed. By April 6, the 179th was hard at work evacuating three thousand five hundred prisoners of war taken in just a few days. Because transport vehicles were in such demand for hauling supplies and men, when some German soldiers threw down their weapons and raised their arms, American troops took the weapons and ordered them to march to the rear. The Americans didn't want to spare a fighting man to guard prisoners.

On April 12, there came a report that gave all pause: Franklin D. Roosevelt was dead.

"In the foxholes of Germany there was shock, disbelief, silence," the regimental history of the 179th regiment noted. "The American soldier had lost his [Commander in Chief] on the threshold of final victory. But more than that, he had lost his greatest exponent of humanity and peace, his spokesman for order and sanity in the coming chaos of the post war world. He had lost the man who knew what he was fighting for."

In response, the 45th Division seemed to fight with increased fury, according to the regimental history: "The Germans countered with flak wagon fire, machine gun fire and every field gun they could hurriedly bring up. Their infantry fought stubbornly."

And then came German jets, aircraft so fast that Allied anti-aircraft guns were useless. "In one moment American bombers glittered in the sunlight overhead, droning on toward their targets, in the next, three were hurtling down to death and two jet-propelled enemy aircraft were already disappearing — specks in the blue," the regimental history noted.

It was perhaps part of one final, if loud, gasp. According to Allied Intelligence, Hitler was likely consolidating his remaining troops and armaments. American troops felt an urgency to drive through southern Germany, reach Munich, and capture Hitler before he and his generals could make one last and certainly bloody stand.

CHAPTER 11

THE 179TH INFANTRY PLOWED AHEAD, TAKING HOXHOHL, Alsbach, Jugenheim, and Seeheim. But then, the men came face-to-face with Aschaffenburg, a city so heavily defended that some journalists called it the "Little Siegfried Line."

The battle for Aschaffenburg was a six-day siege that ultimately left a historic and picturesque city in rubble. Soldiers would later recall being able to stand in the city center and see beyond the city limits. The buildings, church spires, and towers were gone.

In Aschaffenburg, American soldiers came up against fanatical teenage boys willing to fight to the death. The city was controlled by a German major who ordered that any civilian residents trying to flee be machine-gunned down. Many were.

Some German officers who sought to surrender were publicly hanged. One German lieutenant was strung up in front of a wine shop, his hands bound behind him. A sign hung from his neck: "Cowards and traitors hang!"

The city fell on April 3, and thousands of German soldiers were taken prisoner. The high-ranking officers who had overseen the carnage withdrew before they could be captured.

From mid-March to the end of the battle for Aschaffenburg, the 45th Division took nearly twenty thousand German soldiers prisoner and killed or wounded more than thirty-three thousand.

On April 9 Teen Palm wrote his mother.

I am sitting in a German courtyard underneath a beautiful warm sun, taking it easy. All around me are broken German weapons and helmets plus shell holes in the clock tower overhead. We have been pushing fast and hard ever since crossing the Rhine. I have ridden tanks, ducks and artillery trucks fighting from town to town.

I hope you all had a nice Easter with plenty of good warm weather. I am hoping this can keep up so the war can come to a more speedy end.

While the 157th Infantry Division remained to mop up in Aschaffenburg, the 179th and 180th Infantry divisions kept on the move. Ahead lay the heart of Nazi Germany. Nuremberg, where in the 1930s the Nazi Party held giant conventions, was about sixty-five miles southeast of Aschaffenburg, and less than thirty-five miles beyond Nuremberg was Munich.

Palm and his men trudged through woods and roads softened into mire by spring rain, managing to cross fourteen miles, halting near Obersinn. Over ten days they fought through Volkers, Speicherz, and Kothen, encountering less opposition as they advanced.

Swinging directly south, they moved through Bamberg and then on to Nuremberg, which they secured on April 20. The fighting was fierce. According to *The Fighting Forty-Fifth*, a history of the division compiled and edited by a number of officers,

Many of the prisoners taken had to be routed from basements, tunnels and air raid shelters. From windows, wine cellars, and piles of debris in the desolate wreckage-strewn streets, the snipers continued to operate against the tired and dust-covered Americans ... Soldiers told of fighting against children ... boys of 14 years old who sniped at Americans or threw hand grenades.

Continuing south, Palm and his men came to the swift-moving Danube River, the last significant physical barrier between them and Munich.

On April 25, a German general who had been captured by the Allies issued a plea for Hitler to stop the fighting.

Speaking in German in a broadcast aired on Luxembourg radio, the officer said he was addressing the German high command to "make the Fuehrer cease fighting at once" because "the war is irrevocably lost."

"It is your duty," he declared, "to stop this senseless slaughter of our youth and destruction of our best cities. You must succeed in making reason conquer against military amateurs."

His entreaty was ignored.

It is very unlikely that Palm heard that broadcast, though by then he certainly would have agreed that the war had indeed become a senseless slaughter, not just of Germans, but of mankind. Indeed, the truth of those words soon would be seared into his soul.

By the following morning, the 179th Infantry controlled the north bank of the river near Neuberg. The 179th had traveled four hundred miles in the month since crossing the Rhine. The crossing of the Danube was set for 3:00 p.m., and assault boats were brought to its bank by engineers. Scouts had stealthily crossed the river the night before and returned without drawing enemy fire. They reported that the men could expect little or no German resistance.

Captain Robertson and Palm were in one of the boats as it began motoring across the river. Despite the scouting report, the soldiers were tense because of their potential exposure to enemy fire during the long minutes they sat unprotected in the boats. But there was no fire on the pontoon boats as they approached the shoreline. For the moment, the Germans did not appear to be contesting the water crossing.

As the boats grounded just short of land, Palm and Robertson and their men leaped out and began wading ashore. Among their number was a young Polish teenager whom the soldiers of Company B had encountered while moving between Aschaffenburg and Nuremberg.

One of the soldiers there that day, Lieutenant Robert M. Barnhart, later recalled that some men in the unit had taken the Pole to Robertson. In broken English, the young man said he had escaped from a German prison. He didn't want any money, he said. All he wanted was a rifle and a helmet and a chance to kill Germans.

Robertson yielded to the Pole's entreaty. The young man proved his mettle in firefights during the next several days and quickly became emotionally attached to Robertson.

They crossed the Danube without a single shot being fired. Then, as Palm and Robertson were about to set foot on solid ground, there was the loud crack of a rifle shot.

Robertson dropped straight down, his body lying half in the water, half on shore. He was dead before his body had landed. A single bullet had struck him right between his eyes.

The other men hit the ground and scrambled for cover. They waited, but there were no more shots. Gripping his rifle tightly, Palm allowed himself a glance at Robertson's body.

The man Palm had so admired as the best superior he had ever served was still. Waves lapped at his uniform. The current tugged at the body, as if to carry it away.

Suddenly, about a dozen German soldiers stepped out from behind clumps of bushes where they had been hiding. They threw down their rifles and helmets in surrender. They raised their arms above their heads.

Palm rose to his feet, soaking wet, filled with rage and sorrow. But he was able to realize his heavy responsibility, and he forced himself to act, to speak. He ordered a sergeant: "Take a look at those rifles. I want to know who fired that shot."

The sergeant motioned for the Germans to pick up their guns. Nervously, they complied. Methodically, the sergeant walked from man to man, sniffing the gun barrels of each of the weapons. When he was finished, he grabbed one of the rifles, turned to face Palm and said, solemnly, "Just this one, sir. This is the one."

The Germans were silent, likely fearful they were all about to be killed. Death was no stranger to any of these men gathered at the banks of the river, to any men in battle. All of these men had seen friends and foes die in enormous numbers.

This was war, they had been told, and they had all been constantly counseled not to get too friendly with their comrades, told that emotional attachments would prove a hindrance and would sap the will and efficiency of the fighting man. But there was no way to erase the proclivity to bond in these horrible conditions. Such is the way of the human spirit. Living in foxholes and fighting side by side, covering for one another, and protecting one another brought men together. It did not drive them apart.

No matter how many of their comrades were shot, shattered, or blown to unrecognizable pieces, men could not erase or suppress the emotion of seeing a friend, fellow soldier, or respected and admired leader gunned down before their eyes.

And so at that moment, with the only sound the rhythmic lapping of the river's waves, a decision was made. It may have been verbal. It may have been tacit, unspoken, communicated with a curt nod of Teen Palm's head.

And the Polish teenager moved. He walked toward the owner of the offending weapon. Gesturing toward the water with his M-1 rifle, the Pole moved toward the bank. Slowly, the German began wading into the water, facing the far side of the river.

When he was waist-deep, the Pole, his face contorted and his voice raw, cried out in German for the soldier to turn around: *"Umdrehen!"*

His feet shifting as he fought against the river's current, the German obeyed the command and turned, his arms at his sides. Wordlessly and deliberately, the Pole raised his rifle, aimed, and pulled the trigger. He emptied the magazine. Eight shots pierced the German's midsection. Almost in slow motion, the soldier's body slid sideways and was swept downstream in a swirl of blood.

Tears welled in Palm's eyes as he knelt beside Robertson's body, the sounds of gunshots still echoing in his head. Silently, he prayed, and all around him was silence.

Eventually, he rose and he spoke aloud. He ordered the men, now his men, to secure Robertson's body for removal to the rear, along with the remaining German prisoners.

And then, he and his men moved on.

CHAPTER 12

AFTER SUCCESSFUL CROSSINGS OF THE RHINE, THE ALLIED armies pushed steadily to the east and north against retreating German forces. By late March, it appeared that General Eisenhower was likely to order the forces on to capture Berlin before the Russian Red Army could do so. But no such order came.

Much to the disappointment of English Prime Minister Winston Churchill and British Field Marshall Bernard Montgomery, Eisenhower decided that Munich and Bavaria, not Berlin, would be the chief objectives of the Allied troops. He proposed that the Russian Army drive toward the Allied forces and split Germany in half. The Russians would then move north and capture Berlin, while significant Allied forces would head south towards Munich, the birthplace of the Nazi Party and, since 1934, hailed as the capital city of the movement.

Eisenhower believed this strategy would deliver a knockout blow against Hitler very quickly and thus save Allied lives. He foresaw that capturing Berlin would be costly. In fact, the Russians would incur more than three hundred and fifty thousand casualties (killed, wounded, or ill) in the Battle for Berlin.

Eisenhower's reasoning was based in part on a particular map that hung on the wall in the map room in the offices of the Supreme Headquarters of the Allied Expeditionary Force in Reims, France. This room, located near Eisenhower's office, contained a chart that depicted the National Redoubt, twenty thousand square miles of mountainous wooded terrain where some intelligence sources said Hitler planned to make his last stand.

Authors Ada Petrova and Peter Watson, in their book *The Death of Hitler: The Full Story with New Evidence from Secret Russian Archives*, detailed how the map was updated to show a growing presence of Nazi forces there.

The National Redoubt map was covered in red marks, each one a military symbol denoting this or that defense installation. A Y meant a radio transmitter, a square stood for barracks, a crescent with an F inside indicated a food dump. There were signs for ammunition stores, for petrol and chemical warfare dumps and for underground factories. Fortified positions were shown with zigzag lines. Every day more symbols were added to the chart, so much so that this mountain defense system, the National Redoubt, seemed [to the Allied command] the greatest remaining threat in the European war, greater even than the prize of Berlin.

It was in this Alpine area, according to Allied intelligence, that the Nazis intended to make their last stand, with Adolf Hitler at their head. The terrain was so difficult as to be almost impregnable but, again according to intelligence, the remaining Nazi leadership would not be content merely to sit back and absorb whatever the Allies could throw at them. A new type of commando unit had been created, called the Werewolves, whose task it was to sneak out from the Redoubt and create mayhem among the occupation armies. Some 200,000 veteran troops and Werewolves were to cover an area of 20,000 square miles, it was rumored, to Bavaria, Austria and a small part of Italy.

In late March, according to Petrova and Martin, intelligence reports filed with the Seventh Army, which included Teen Palm's unit, "described an elite force of mainly SS and mountain troops at least 200,000 to 300,000 strong. The reports said that up to five very long trains were arriving in the Redoubt area every week and that new types of weapons had been observed on these trains." An underground factory was believed to be manufacturing Messerschmitt fighter planes.

The Allied command believed that the Nazis were consolidating significant command personnel in the Redoubt. The command believed that Hermann Goering, head of the German Air Force, Hitler's confidant and the man designated as his successor; Heinrich Himmler, head of the SS; and Hitler were "in the process of withdrawing to their respective personal mountain strongholds."

In the early morning hours of April 16, 1945, Soviet leader Joseph Stalin launched "Operation Berlin." The capture of Berlin constituted his supreme goal. The Battle for Berlin, one of the bloodiest struggles of the war, entered a new phase four days later. A Berlin mother, huddled in her basement, wrote in her diary: "Friday, April 20th, was Hitler's fifty-sixth birthday, and the Soviets sent him a birthday present in the form of an artillery barrage right into the heart of the city, while the Western Allies joined in with a massive air raid." The city was pounded around the clock by Soviet artillery, and after a week, Berlin was surrounded by Russian troops, tanks, and artillery. The fighting was extremely ferocious. Russian tanks, accompanied by teams of veteran street fighters, moved from building to building on the outskirts of Berlin and began to move steadfastly toward the center of the city. An estimated five hundred thousand German soldiers, some of them young boys, were said to be fighting to the death.

Stalin announced that Unter den Linden, once the most famous street in the city's most historic section, was a smoking ruin. Russian troops were a little more than a mile away and still advancing.

Some dispatches from Moscow said the Soviets believed that Hitler and his staff were still in Berlin. One report indicated that Russian soldiers were "scouring every inch of overrun territory inside the Reich capital in the hope that Adolf Hitler might be found." He was presumed to be operating in a heavily fortified building and personally directing the defense of the city.

That could not be confirmed, however, and some high-ranking officers believed the Soviets were relying on propaganda reports designed to keep the German Army fighting. Others believed that Hitler had already left Berlin to avoid being captured by the Russians.

Newspapers across the United States carried reports describing the quest to find Hitler. "Where's Der Fuehrer?" read one headline. "Giant Manhunt on for Hitler" read another. Independent News Service reporter Charles A. Smith filed a report datelined April 24 that breathlessly described the search:

> There were increasing indications today that the greatest manhunt in history, over land and thru the air was

developing in search of Adolf Hitler. Few persons give any credence to Nazi propaganda claims that Hitler is in Berlin, as proclaimed by Propaganda Minister Joseph Goebbels at the start of the battle for the Reich capital and repeated daily by the German radio.

Smith described Soviet "vengeance planes" patrolling day and night in case the Nazis were to put an escape plane into the sky.

The British Foreign Office reported that they believed Hitler was in the Redoubt. "Altho no one knows positively, it is believed there was an even chance that he was at Berchtesgaden and at least got a thoro shaking up by the huge RAF missiles capable of deep penetration," Smith reported. "Repeat raids on key points in the Redoubt and on Berchtesgaden are eagerly anticipated in London. RAF pilots were reported vying for the honor to continue such maneuvers."

Smith was referring to bombing runs by more than 350 English Royal Air Force planes that dumped tons of bombs in the Redoubt and specifically on the Berghof and the "Eagle's Nest," two of Hitler's mountain retreats located near Berchtesgaden.

"Hitler's Mountain House Destroyed by British Bomb," screamed one headline. "Adjoining Eagle's Nest Damaged and Barracks of Dictator's Bodyguard Smashed in Raid — Whether Fuehrer Was at Scene Is Unknown."

On April 26, Allen Dulles, the chief intelligence officer on Germany for the U.S., radioed his superiors in Washington, D.C., that the whereabouts of Hitler and Heinrich Himmler, the architect of the Holocaust, were unknown. "A few days ago," Dulles reported, "they were both in or near Berlin. Have they remained there, to go down in ruins, or have they got away by plane? This is a question we can't answer.

"With the sky patrol of ... American and Russian planes in this area, the retreat by air during recent days would have been a hazardous job," he said. "It is conceivable that Hitler will just disappear and that we will never know definitely what has become of him. This will give his fanatical followers the possibility of continuing to use his name to keep alive the underground movement."

Hitler had come to personify evil. Millions of people had lost their lives, and millions more had suffered untold agony and destruction under his command.

While some Allied leaders wanted to capture him and put him on trial for crimes against humanity, others suggested that would be a waste of time. Churchill, believing such a trial would be a sham, had suggested that Hitler be executed like a gangster in an electric chair, going so far as to suggest that they might borrow "Old Sparky," the name commonly used to refer to the electric chair in the United States.

Capturing Hitler alive and keeping him alive, though, could provide a wealth of intelligence to the Allies, including the locations of secret caches of weapons, particularly lethal poison gas.

Allied troops were focused on Munich — Hitler's favorite city and the place where he and his brown shirts had forged the Nazi Party. Hitler reveled in the city's architecture, its music and its Bavarian customs. Here, too, was the Brown House, the national headquarters of the Nazi Party where Hitler and other high Nazi officials maintained offices.

Now, as never before, the search for Hitler was intensifying. With no one able to dissuade Hitler from continuing to wage war, only his capture or his death could end it.

CHAPTER 13

STEADILY, THE ALLIED FORCES MOVED FORWARD. BY LATE April they were within thirty miles of Munich. Eagerly awaiting their arrival was a twenty-nine-year-old German Army officer named Rupprecht Gerngross.

Gerngross had been born in Shanghai to German parents. The family moved to Munich following World War I. He later studied at the London School of Economics and earned a law degree.

Gerngross, like all German males, was required to serve in the German Army. After the war broke out in 1939, he was among German troops that marched into Poland. After three weeks, he was outside of Lemberg when a sniper hiding behind a tombstone shot him in the upper thigh. He was taken by truck to a field hospital in Jaroslaw.

While he was recuperating, he learned that Nazi SS troops were searching the occupied territory, looking for members of the Polish resistance and Jews. One afternoon, he was drawn to the window of his room by the sound of gunshots. When he looked out, he could see a group of people in dark robes lining up in front of a garbage dump.

He could also see a line of soldiers and recognized them by their uniforms as SS troops. Suddenly, the soldiers raised their weapons and fired a thunderous salvo. Most of the robed figures dropped immediately. Some staggered and were then felled by more gunfire. The bodies were rolled into the dump and covered with dirt.

Jews are being executed, Gerngross realized. Hitler had brought mass murder to his regime. The event was seared into Gerngross's brain.

Two years later, Gerngross was sent to the Russian front. By then he was a first lieutenant commanding an artillery platoon. Leading his platoon on horseback, an exploding grenade felled his horse, pinning Gerngross underneath. When soldiers dragged the horse away, Gerngross appeared lifeless. When a sergeant pressed his face up close, he realized that Gerngross was alive but unable to speak. In response to the sergeant's questions, Gerngross blinked to show that he was not dead.

Mortar and grenades began to explode around them, and the sergeant hastily took off his coat and covered Gerngross. He promised to send an ambulance and left to take over command and lead the platoon forward.

When night came, Gerngross was still alone, too weak to move. As he lay praying for help, he thought of the Jews he had seen executed in Poland. He wondered if some of them were still alive when the clods of dirt were shoveled over them. At that moment, he concluded the real enemies were not the Russians, but the Nazis.

As he would say later, he had not become a soldier to fight for "this Germany" — a nation that would perpetrate such massacres. From this moment forward, he began secretly working against the barbarous Nazis as part of the German resistance movement.

In the early morning hours, rescuers found him and took

him for medical treatment. After four weeks, he was released from the hospital, but he was not sent back to the front. Although he had recovered, he was not physically fit enough to return to the battle and so was assigned to oversee an interpreter unit in Munich.

There he discretely began recruiting members of this unit to join him in a plot to overthrow the Nazis in Munich. On one occasion, when he learned that one of his best students was going to be shipped to the front, Gerngross broke into a superior's office and forged the student's record to show that he had a medical condition that would prevent him from being sent into battle.

One of Gerngross's allies was Jürgen Wittenstein, who belonged to the Munich-based White Rose, a group of mostly medical students who were drawn together initially by their shared interests in the arts, music, literature, and philosophy. Many of them also had Jewish friends or classmates who had been deported. Wittenstein had entered the military in 1937 and by the spring of 1939 was enrolled as a medical student at the University of Munich, where he befriended several other students who would become the heart of the White Rose.

After the invasion of Poland that fall, as news of atrocities there emerged and with the deportations of Jews continuing, some university students became convinced that they had to take action.

In the summer of 1942, the White Rose circulated four typed leaflets that called upon German citizens to engage in active resistance, including acts of sabotage against the Nazi regime for engaging in "the most abominable tyranny our people has ever endured." The leaflets, which specifically denounced the extermination of Jews, were left in telephone books inside public telephone booths, sent to professors and students, and couriered to other universities for distribution. Mere possession of a leaflet was a crime that carried the death penalty.

At the time, Paul Giesler was one of the most powerful figures in Munich. Giesler had long been a prominent member of the Nazi Party and had been involved in planning the invasions of Poland and France. In 1942, he was named the head of the German state of Bavaria and was also appointed to a political position known as *gauleiter*, which conferred on him what was essentially dictatorial power over southern Germany, including Munich.

In January 1943, all university students were summoned to a convocation at the German Museum in Munich. There Giesler gave an address in which he admonished female students for wasting time attending the university and suggested their true duty was to bear sons for the Fatherland. When some women tried to leave in protest, they were arrested.

In February, German troops in Stalingrad surrendered to the Russians. The battle of Stalingrad lasted two hundred days and is considered the bloodiest battle in human history. Hitler refused Stalin's offer for an honorable surrender, and that decision resulted in more than four hundred thousand German soldiers killed, wounded, or taken prisoner. Most of those captured would die in prison camps.

The students took to the streets. They spent three nights painting anti-Nazi slogans such as "Down with Hitler" and "Hitler — Mass Murderer" on buildings in Munich, including the university.

On February 18, 1943, University of Munich students Sophie Scholl, a biology and philosophy major, and her brother, Hans Scholl, a medical student, went to the university and began distributing stacks of another leaflet outside lecture halls.

This sixth leaflet had been written by university professor Kurt Huber. It decried the deaths at Stalingrad and declared that a day of reckoning had arrived — "... the reckoning of our German youth with the most abominable tyranny our people has ever endured," Huber wrote. "In the name of the entire German people we demand of Adolf Hitler ... the return of personal freedom, the most precious treasure of the Germans which he cunningly has cheated us out of."

After distributing the leaflets outside lecture halls, the Scholls, as a final act, climbed to the top landing of a glass-roofed inner courtyard and dumped a shower of them. They were spotted by a janitor, who summoned authorities, and both were arrested. When Hans Scholl was taken into custody, the Gestapo found in his pocket a draft of a leaflet written by a friend, Christoph Probst, and so Probst was arrested as well.

Four days later, all three were found guilty of treason by Hitler's Peoples Court and within hours were beheaded. Professor Huber and two other medical students, Willi Graf and Alexander Schmorell, subsequently were arrested and put to death for their involvement in the White Rose.

In all, nearly eighty students and sympathizers were taken into custody. Among them were chemistry students Marie-Luise Jahn and Hans Leipelt, both acquaintances of Wittenstein's.

After the executions of the Scholls and Probst, Jahn and Leipelt had begun reproducing the sixth leaflet on a typewriter with a new heading: "Despite Everything, Their Spirit Lives On!" These were distributed in Munich and Hamburg. Some were later obtained and reproduced by the Royal Air

Force and dropped by the thousands over Germany. Jahn and Leipelt were arrested in October as they were collecting money for Huber's widow.

Wittenstein sought out a lawyer to defend Jahn. Although the lawyer managed to get Jahn's death sentence commuted to twelve years in a labor camp, Leipelt was not as fortunate. He was convicted and executed.

At the time Wittenstein sought the services of the lawyer, he was introduced to another lawyer in the office: Rupprecht Gerngross. There, Wittenstein learned of Gerngross's hatred for the Nazis.

Gerngross explained that he was forming a resistance group, Freedom Action Bavaria (FAB). He deeply hoped to prevent the destruction of Munich — a fate that Berlin was facing as the Russian Army converged on the nation's capital and a fate that several other German cities had already suffered.

He believed that with sufficient support, they could trigger an uprising as Allied troops approached Munich. If the Allies were close enough to reach Munich before the Nazis could suppress the revolt, Gerngross believed he and his group could surrender Munich to the Allies and then the entire nation would capitulate, bringing the war to an end.

Wittenstein offered his support immediately.

After the executions of the Scholls and Probst, the Gestapo had questioned Wittenstein extensively in an attempt to link him to the White Rose. It had also questioned Wittenstein's superior officer, who, at great risk, stood up for him.

Though he hadn't been arrested, Wittenstein believed he was under Gestapo surveillance. Unable to flee Germany, he volunteered to go to battle because the Gestapo had no jurisdiction there. He reasoned that being on the front line was safer than staying in Munich and risking his life at the hands of the Gestapo.

A physician, Wittenstein was sent to a makeshift Army hospital in an abandoned train tunnel south of the Po Valley near the Italian front. He was the only physician overseeing medics and nurses treating German wounded.

Secretly, he began to collect the weapons of soldiers who were so badly wounded that they would not be sent back into battle. When Wittenstein had stockpiled a sufficient number of guns and grenades, he sent a coded message to a Gerngross ally and an emissary was dispatched to smuggle the weapons to Munich.

By early 1945, Gerngross had enlisted about four hundred supporters in his effort to save Munich from total destruction. Their numbers included civilians as well as interpreter soldiers, many of whom in their pre-military days were musicians, writers, artists, language students, and teachers.

Although he didn't realize it at the time, there was ample reason for concern. About six weeks earlier, Hitler had issued a scorched-earth order, "Demolitions on Reich Territory," later known as the Nero Decree after the Roman emperor who reigned when Rome was devastated by a massive fire. Hitler ordered the destruction of German transport and communication facilities, factories, and supply depots to keep them out of enemy hands. The destruction of Munich, part of which was already severely damaged by Allied bombing, appeared inevitable.

Paul Giesler, the *gauleiter*, summoned an aide, Bertus Gerdes, to his office in mid-April. Giesler said he had received a directive from Hitler calling for the immediate liquidation of the concentration camp at Dachau and two Jewish labor camps in Landsberg and Mueldorf. Giesler ordered Gerdes to destroy the two labor camps by sending the German Air Force to drop bombs.

Gerdes was not involved in the German resistance, but still, he was horrified. He tried to stall taking action. In response to messages from Berlin, he reported variously that the weather was bad and planes were grounded, or that gasoline and bombs were scarce.

So the plan was changed. The Gestapo was ordered to kill the prisoners at Mueldorf. The Jews at Landsberg were to be marched to the nearby camp at Dachau. Everyone in Dachau, with the exception of Aryan nationals from Western Europe, was to be poisoned.

Gerdes persuaded Giesler to halt that plan by arguing that the Allied troops were so close to Dachau that a mass slaughter might be discovered as it was being carried out. A new directive was issued stating that all Western European prisoners at Dachau were to be transported to Switzerland and the remaining inmates moved to Tyrol where they would be killed.

On April 27, Gerdes fled Munich. But Giesler remained and the threat of destruction loomed. He ordered that Munich be defended to the last man, and in the event the city was going to be overrun by the Allies, its bridges, electrical lines, and water pumping systems were to be destroyed.

Gerngross, meanwhile, spent many months carefully organizing the FAB revolt. He well understood the consequences of failure to members of the German resistance, some of whom had tried to kill Hitler.

There had been several failed attempts to assassinate Hitler in 1943 and 1944. One plot involved placing a bomb on a plane carrying Hitler, but the bomb failed to detonate. In other attempts, resistance members tried to get close enough to kill Hitler with guns, grenades, or bombs. They failed because increasingly, Hitler surrounded himself with a heavy security detail and his movements were kept secret from all but a few of his trusted confidants. He believed divine providence protected him.

One of the assassination attempts involved Gerngross himself.

In January 1944, Gerngross learned covertly that Hitler was headed by automobile to his retreat in Bavaria. Gerngross knew the aide who was Hitler's driver. The man was a resident of Munich, and Gerngross speculated that if Hitler passed through his beloved Munich, the car would stop at the aide's home to allow him a brief visit with his wife and young daughter.

At the time, Gerngross was living in a home across the street from where the aide lived.

He decided to kill Hitler.

Gerngross hid in the attic of his home, waiting for the Fuehrer's car to arrive. For hours he camped in the attic, keeping his eyes on the home and his hands on a rifle fitted with a scope.

Then, at about noon, a Mercedes drew up to the curb. Two men in uniforms emerged. One stood at the side of the car and the other positioned himself near the door of the home. Seconds later, a second Mercedes arrived and pulled up behind the first car.

Gerngross shouldered the rifle, curled his finger around the trigger, and squinted into the scope.

A man in uniform emerged from the second car and opened the front passenger door. The aide who lived in the home got out and walked into the house. Gerngross could make out another figure sitting in the back of the car.

Was it Hitler? he thought. *It had to be Hitler.*

Gerngross took a deep breath and waited.

After several minutes, a young blonde girl, the aide's daughter, came out wearing a Hitler Youth uniform. She ran to the rear of the second car and waved through the window. The guard opened the door and Gerngross could see movement. A man — *Hitler? It had to be Hitler* — stepped out of the car and crouched down so the girl could embrace him around the neck.

Gerngross aimed, waiting for the girl to pull away. The girl stood between Hitler and the barrel of the rifle. Gerngross was sweating. His body tensed.

Hitler caressed the girl's cheek. The crosshairs were aimed at the back of the girl's head. If she moved, Gerngross would pull the trigger twice — one bullet for the head, the second for Hitler's chest.

Suddenly, the aide emerged from the house and Hitler immediately pulled away from the girl and slid back into the car. The aide climbed in, as did the soldiers.

Just that quickly, the opportunity vanished.

Both cars sped off, leaving Gerngross alone with his bitter disappointment.

Months later, another attempt nearly succeeded. On July 20, 1944, Claus von Stauffenberg, a German Army colonel, attended a briefing session with Hitler and other high-ranking Nazi leaders in the Wolf's Lair, Hitler's headquarters near Rastenburg. Von Stauffenberg placed a briefcase containing a bomb with a timer under a conference table and excused himself from the meeting. When the bomb went off, Hitler was partially shielded from the blast by a table leg. He suffered only minor injuries, but several there died of their wounds.

In the wake of the failed attempt, known as Operation Valkyrie, the Gestapo arrested several thousand people and put them on trial. Hitler said he wanted to see the guilty hanging like carcasses in a slaughterhouse. Hundreds were executed, including von Stauffenberg.

Since then, Gerngross had bided his time, preparing and waiting for what he believed was inevitable: the arrival of the Allies on Munich's front doorstep. He did not want to make the same mistakes evident in Operation Valkyrie — a conspiracy with which he was intimately familiar.

Gerngross knew that his small band could not defeat all the Nazi supporters in Munich. But, he reasoned, if the Allied forces were close enough to the city, the uprising could be timed so that the superior numbers and weapons of Allied troops would prevail before the surprised Nazis could halt their entry or stop the FAB revolt.

In preparation, armbands were made for FAB members so they would not be confused with regular German troops. Ambulances were hidden in a garage. Weapons had been stockpiled. Two light tanks commanded by a German lieutenant were stashed and ready to transport Gerngross and a small armed group to a radio station for the takeover. FAB members had secretly moved through the streets of Munich for weeks, defusing explosives that had been planted by the Nazis on the city's bridges.

According to Gerngross's plan, the revolt was to begin with him broadcasting a code word — *"Fasanenjagd"* (pheasant hunting). The word was a reference to *"Goldfasane,"* (golden pheasant), a term of derision attached to high-ranking Nazi military officers flaunting their golden military decorations. The hope was to take out as many high-ranking Nazis as possible. In effect, they would declare open season on the Nazis, such as Giesler. Gerngross believed the broadcast would have a wide audience because everyone with a radio kept it on during the night to be able to hear bombing alerts.

The uprising was designed not only to eliminate Nazi rule in Munich, but to reach out and make peace with the Allies, restore order to the city, and reestablish the rule of law in an attempt to restore basic human rights. A statement of these ideals would be broadcast in the hope that all those opposed to the Nazis would support the revolt.

As the Allies approached, Gerngross dispatched two German officers who were part of FAB to surrender to Allied troops and alert them of the planned uprising. When there was no response, he realized these emissaries and their information had been received with skepticism and suspicion or ignored entirely. Gerngross knew he needed a better plan.

CHAPTER 14

ON APRIL 27, 1945, TEEN PALM HAD BEEN COMMANDER OF his unit for less than twenty-four hours when he was summoned to an unusual meeting of platoon commanders and other officers. More than a dozen men, haggard and unshaven, gathered in the late afternoon.

Two days earlier, an American airman had arrived from Munich, accompanied by a German soldier. The American brought a strange and almost unbelievable request. Please, he asked, do not bomb Munich for the next forty-eight hours.

Who was this man? And why would an American want to halt the bombing of Munich? His name was Bernard McNamara, and nearly two years earlier, at 11:00 a.m. on October 20, 1943, he was riding in one of nineteen American B-17 bombers that roared to life and rumbled down the runway of the Molesworth, England, air base and soared into the sky. The Flying Fortresses each carried ten five-hundred-pound bombs and were headed for Duren, Germany, to drop their payload on the center of the city.

The base was the home of the 303rd Bombardment Group, an Eighth Air Force B-17 bomber group that had been launching bombing missions since 1942. This was the 303rd's seventy-ninth mission.

Strapped in the navigator's seat of the bomber, twenty-four-year-old Second Lieutenant McNamara was calm as the plane rose above the English Channel. This was the twenty-fourth mission he had flown with the pilot, John W. Hendry Jr., and each time they had returned safely to their base. It was his twenty-fifth mission overall — and completing it meant he would qualify to return home. This mission, though, would be his last.

As the nineteen-plane formation crossed the French coast, as many as a dozen Luftwaffe Messerschmitt fighter planes ambushed them, bursting out of a bank of clouds about five hundred yards from the lead B-17. The Messerschmitts zoomed in with cannons blazing and hit McNamara's plane in the left wing.

Flames erupted and Hendry quickly assessed the problem — the plane was loaded with fuel and a catastrophic explosion was likely just moments away. Indeed, he could see another of the group's planes spinning in flames as it hurtled toward the ground.

Hendry was able to put the plane in a controlled descent and gave the order to bail out. One by one, eight members of the ten-man crew leaped from the burning craft and popped open their parachutes. They were not safe yet — they were over German-controlled territory.

As McNamara drifted down, suspended from his chute, a German plane swooped toward him, machine guns firing. McNamara was hit in the head — the bullet pierced his face below his right eye and exited under his chin. He also was struck in his left arm and left thigh. He crashed into the roof of an auto repair shop in Sauve, a suburb of Valenciennes, France. Local residents hauled him down and took him to a nearby home.

They put him on the floor near a fire to keep him warm. A doctor was summoned and began patching his wounds.

Two hours later, though, German troops on patrol — drawn to the home by a crowd of French residents that had gathered to see an American — found him and took him prisoner.

Two of the crew did not get out of the plane and were still on board when it crashed. Second Lieutenant William B. Harper and Technical Sergeant James J. Brown were found dead in the wreckage. The other members of the crew — Hendry, Second Lieutenant Richard E. Webster, Technical Sergeant Alfred J. Hargrave, Sergeant Delbert E. Guhr, Staff Sergeant Wilmer G. Raesley, Technical Sergeant Loran C. Biddle, and Staff Sergeant John Doherty — managed to reach the ground alive. All were captured by German troops.

McNamara was taken to a Luftwaffe hospital for further treatment. Three months later, when he was able to walk, he was transferred to Stalag Luft III South, a prison compound in Poland where other Allied airmen were held prisoner.

In March 1944, seventy-six British flyers fled the camp through a tunnel in a break that was famously depicted in the book and film *The Great Escape.* All but three were captured within two days, some of them as they waited for a train headed toward Alsace, France, and, they hoped, freedom. Returned to the camp, fifty of the seventy-three were executed.

In April 1945, McNamara was among a number of other prisoners who managed to escape from the prison with the assistance of a German soldier in the camp who accepted a bribe of cigarettes to allow McNamara to walk out of the camp and ride off on a bicycle that had been stashed nearby. Following a hand-drawn map, McNamara rode to a nearby farm, where he connected with a group of Serbians who were actively attempting to get an American to Munich to help Gerngross communicate with the Allies about his planned uprising.

From there, McNamara was driven variously by car and truck toward Munich, traveling twenty to thirty kilometers at a stretch. On the night of April 21, McNamara slept in a trailer full of straw, and on the following morning he hid in a water main until a car arrived from Munich. Then he was driven to the home of mechanic George Roedter. By day, Roedter worked on German Army vehicles. Secretly, though, he was a member of Gerngross's FAB. For many months, Roedter had allowed his home to be used as a hiding place for escaped prisoners of war as they made their way back to the protection of the Allies. Many of these escapees had been helped by Gerngross's interpreter unit.

As the Allies approached Munich, Gerngross decided that the only credible emissary he could send to reveal his planned uprising, and to ask that the bombing of Munich be halted was an American.

So he went to see George Roedter.

There, Gerngross found McNamara and Sidney Leigh, a twenty-four-year-old lieutenant from New Jersey, whose bomber had been shot down in July 1943 over Kassel, Germany. Like McNamara, he had been taken prisoner by the Nazis. Shuffled from one prison camp to another, Leigh wound up in Stalag VII A, north of Moosburg in Bavaria, Germany. Like McNamara, he escaped, made his way to Munich, and was taken by German resistance members to Roedter's home.

Gerngross outlined his plan for the revolt and asked Leigh to help the FAB kidnap Franz von Epp, a seventy-six-year-old man of considerable power and influence in the Nazi Party. Gerngross believed that the chance of a successful revolt would increase if he could persuade von Epp to make a public plea urging German soldiers to put down their arms.

When Gerngross proposed that FAB supporters smuggle an American dressed in a German Army uniform to the Allies so they could be alerted, Leigh suggested McNamara, who was asleep in a rear bedroom.

Roedter awakened McNamara and together they walked into the room where Gerngross waited.

"This is First Lieutenant McNamara," Roedter said.

Speaking in English, Gerngross addressed McNamara, who was still not fully awake.

"I want to send you on a secret mission across the front to your people," he said. "Do you understand?"

McNamara became alert. He did not hesitate.

"Let's go," he replied.

Gerngross explained that McNamara would travel with a French agent and a German from Gerngross's interpreter unit. If stopped by Germans, the German would say he was transporting two Allied prisoners. If they were able to reach the Allies, they were to explain that they were transporting a German prisoner of war.

Gerngross told McNamara that he was to tell the Allies about the planned uprising and that all bombing of Munich should halt so the revolt could begin. After Munich was in the hands of the FAB, Gerngross said, the city would be handed over to the Allies.

Two hours later, McNamara, who was armed with a pistol, departed with the German soldier and the Frenchman, traveling in a small truck carrying three bicycles. Taking back roads, wagon paths, and other obscure byways, they traveled about thirty-five miles north of Munich where they abandoned the truck and struck out on the bicycles.

They traveled through fields and woods to avoid areas still controlled by the German Army. Occasionally they were close enough to roads to see a steady stream of troops falling back in disarray.

They arrived in Neuberg in the early morning hours of April 25 and were taken to a home controlled by the German resistance, where they ate and went to bed. Massive explosions from dropping bombs roused them several hours later. A plane in flames crashed into the building, and a bomb exploded on the street out in front.

With an escort from the resistance, McNamara and his two companions fled the building, running through burning debris on the street to reach a wall that provided protection as they made their way to a bridge. In the chaos of the bombing, they were able to make their way over the bridge without being noticed. They were taken to a German prisoner-of-war camp where a soldier who was sympathetic to the Allies smuggled them inside.

There they remained to wait for the Allies to approach.

They did not have to wait long. Soon, McNamara began hearing the sound of artillery fire. The Allied attack on Neuberg had begun and in a matter of a few hours the city was overrun. Shortly before midnight, McNamara was escorted to the Allies and delivered Gerngross's message.

He reported that Gerngross wanted the Allies to halt all Munich bombing raids for forty-eight hours so the FAB could launch its uprising. McNamara explained that Gerngross believed air attacks would bring German soldiers out in force to clean up the rubble, remove the dead, and treat the wounded, and that for the revolt to succeed, the German Army needed to be caught off guard.

McNamara said Gerngross wanted a signal that the Allies had gotten the message.

In Munich, on the evening of April 26, Leigh began seeing flashes in the night sky that could only be artillery fire — the Allies were approaching.

The following night, at midnight, Gerngross went to Roedter's home, accompanied by Fritz Seiling, von Epp's chief aide who had secretly defected to the FAB. They came to get Leigh to kidnap von Epp.

A few hours earlier, a bomb called a "Christmas Tree" — used to help bombers locate their targets — had been detonated in the skies over the nearby town of Freising. Gerngross witnessed the fiery explosion. He rightly believed this was the sign that the Allies had been informed and had agreed to suspend bombing the city so the FAB revolt could begin.

When he stepped into Roedter's home, Gerngross cut a striking figure. Two submachine guns were strapped across his back. Two pistols were jammed into ammunition belts around his waist. In one hand, he carried a sack of grenades.

Speaking rapidly, he explained to Leigh that he was heading to von Epp's home and wanted Leigh to come along. Gerngross reasoned that von Epp, confronted by an American, would capitulate because he would be convinced that the Nazi cause was doomed.

Leigh agreed, and all three climbed into a waiting car and sped to von Epp's residence. When they arrived, Leigh remained in the car, clutching the bag of hand grenades.

After a short time, Gerngross returned to the car accompanied by von Epp, who climbed into the front seat. They sped off to the private home of an FAB sympathizer outside of Munich where von Epp was put in a separate room.

Gerngross departed and headed for the radio station in

Freimann where he joined twenty FAB commandos armed with submachine guns and other firearms. They overpowered the guards at the radio station and commandeered the microphone. At 2:00 a.m., Gerngross began broadcasting the code word *"Fasanenjagd."* The hunt for the golden pheasants was on.

Teams of FAB members donned their armbands and fanned out in search of specific targets. Five teams set out to find Geisler and kill him. The mission to kill Nazis kicked into gear.

One team invaded the Munich police station and disarmed the police there. Other teams attacked and seized the offices of two newspapers.

FAB member Max Stangl later told *Stars and Stripes* that even before the broadcast began, the Nazi chief of security was walking out of the Ministry of Interior building when three FAB members approached. They asked for his pistol and demanded he sign a resignation letter that Gerngross prepared earlier. After he complied, the men hanged him from a lamppost.

Stangl's assignment was to kill the editor of the Nazi Party newspaper. He went to the man's home wearing a military-hospital sling as if he had been wounded. When he saw the editor come out of his home, Stangl began to feign a limp and started groaning as if in pain.

The man approached and flashed a light on him, demanding to know what was going on. Stangl, who had a pistol in his hand covered up by the sling, shot him three times. When the man fell to the ground, Stangl stood over him and shot him between the eyes for good measure.

At the radio station, Gerngross was broadcasting a lengthy list of entreaties to the city's civilians, politicians, and factory workers as well as municipal employees in charge of transportation and utilities.

Gerngross revealed the existence of the FAB and said the group was putting an end to Nazism in Munich and that the war was over.

"All opponents of National Socialism [Nazis] are summoned to act together and do your part for the common battle and finish off the rest of the Nazis with a death blow. We are fighting against the madness of battle and for the restoration of peace and a democratic system of government."

Government officials, he said, must join in to end the war. "The pompous Nazis have forfeited your rights as a state employee. They are only willing to save their own lives and are willing to sacrifice the whole nation — your wives, your children, as well as the soldiers at the front. Strike the death machine of the Nazis with a death blow," he boomed. "Stay away from your government offices and bring down the machine. Be ready to quickly restore the peace."

Gerngross pleaded with the utility workers to protect their facilities from destruction by the Nazis. "Take over the security of the water and electrical supply. Watch the activity of Nazis known to you and arrest them when they seem to be suspiciously hanging around the facilities. By acting fast, you can save the lives of thousands of people."

He urged the transportation and factory workers to stay home. "Don't go to work. Disrupt transportation when and wherever you can, but be ready to return to normal operation for Freedom Action Bavaria. Do not allow sabotage."

His voice ringing out over the airwaves, Gerngross told the city police to work for the return of order. "You have seen with your eyes the methods of the Party; the consequences of force without boundaries. You also witnessed the ultimate consequences of this brutal power — how the entire German people stand despised all over the world because they forgot themselves and handed themselves over to bloodthirsty tyrants. Give up your work for the Nazis!"

He urged those listening to hang out white flags of surrender, and, sure enough, flags began to appear from windows across the city. Citizens began streaming into the streets, believing the war had come to an end.

A messenger brought news that Allied troops had broken through at Odelzhausen, a small town about thirty miles northwest of Munich noted for a seven-hundred-year-old castle. Gerngross promptly put it on the air.

"The tower of the castle has been hit by Allied grenades and is ablaze!" he thundered. "The Allies are approaching!"

Advancing Allied troops and Radio Luxembourg heard Gerngross's appeal. *Stars and Stripes* printed the headline: "Anti-Nazi Revolt Reported Raging in Munich."

One of the FAB commando teams targeted Giesler and attempted to storm the building where he was hiding. But they fled when confronted by a barrage of hand grenades. Giesler was quickly spirited out of Munich. Three of his brothers were not so fortunate. They all were killed.

In just a few hours, more than a dozen high-ranking Nazis — golden pheasants — were rousted and assassinated. White flags dangled from the building windows. Citizens flocked to the streets, crying, "The war is over!" Rumors circulated that Hitler was dead.

Emboldened by the broadcast, residents of small towns took up arms against the Nazis as well. In Penzberg, about thirty miles south of Munich, Hans Rummer, who had been the town's mayor until he was deposed by the Nazis, gathered men and armed them with handguns. They visited nearby mines and persuaded the pit managers to stop working. They visited a local POW camp and promised imminent liberation, then went to the town's City Hall.

They stormed the building and took over the offices. When the man installed as the mayor by the Nazis came to work, Rummer had him escorted from the building with orders that he leave the city.

Meanwhile, FAB members were working on von Epp, trying to persuade him to go to the radio station and announce the surrender of Munich to the Allies. About 8:00 a.m., Seiling, von Epp's aide, emerged alone from the room and hustled Leigh out of the house to a waiting car. He explained to Leigh that after hours of cajoling, von Epp had seemed to be on the verge of supporting the revolt, but in the end, he stiffened and refused to cooperate.

"Get on the floor," Seiling demanded and tromped on the gas pedal. As they sped off, the aide reached over, turned on the radio, and tuned it to a station in a Munich suburb. Leigh heard a voice shouting and ranting. He knew enough German to understand what was being said.

A man was excoriating Gerngross as a traitor and announcing that the rebels had been defeated — the revolt was over. Gerngross, the voice declared, was to be shot on sight. The voice called on the citizens of Munich to remain loyal to the Fatherland and promised that Gerngross and his supporters would be rounded up and executed.

The voice was that of Paul Giesler.

When word reached Gerngross that Giesler had escaped and that the Allies were not going to reach Munich in time to help his efforts, he and some of his top aides fled the city in a car bearing SS license plates. The radio station was soon back in Nazi control.

German soldiers and members of the Werewolves commandos were soon on the streets, where gun battles raged. As many as one hundred fifty FAB insurgents from Munich and surrounding towns were killed in firefights or captured and then executed. Some were hanged on the street. Others were shot in the woods.

In Penzberg, the Werewolves moved in, disarmed Rummer and his men, and put them under guard. Later that day, on orders from Giesler, Rummer and six others were lined up before a wall and executed by a firing squad. That evening, eight more of Rummer's supporters were arrested and hanged.

In Götting, a Roman Catholic priest named Joseph Grimm was executed. Grimm's crime? After hearing Gerngross on the radio, he removed a Swastika flag from his church and replaced it with a white and blue Bavarian flag.

In the town of Dachau, street fighting broke out between those who heeded Gerngross's appeal and members of the SS. A number of the resistance fighters were slain.

Fritz Seiling, von Epp's aide who had helped in the kidnapping of von Epp, was also executed.

The revolt was over.

Although quashed in a matter of hours, the uprising had inflicted serious damage. The FAB had executed several powerful Nazi leaders and driven Giesler into hiding. The morale of German troops teetered in the face of evidence that defeating Allied forces was an illusion.

Though routed and suffering severe casualties, the FAB did not disappear. Those members who did not flee the city merely hid their armbands and went back to their homes. Some of them were about to meet Teen Palm.

Teen Palm in 1943

Pastor Charles J. Woodbridge's family in Salisbury, North Carolina, 1945, from top left:Charles, Ruth, Rosemary, Norma. Bottom left: Pat, John.

Independent Presbyterian Church,
Savannah, Georgia, late 1940s

Ruth Woodbridge, Teen Palm, and Charles Woodbridge
at Columbia Bible College, 1943

Charles and Ruth
Woodbridge, 1960

The Grand Parade of Adolf Hitler's Wehrmacht
fiftieth birthday on April 20, 1939

Capt. William J. Robertson — Commander, Company B, 179th Infantry, Spring, 1945, in Germany

Prisoners, May 1945

Polish boy liberated from prison
camp in Nuremburg. He had been
imprisioned at age twelve and freed
at age seventeen. He was a bag of bones when found,
but after a few months (seen here) seemed well fed.

Nov 10, 1944

Dearest Glad:

Here I am finally with a letter
to you after all three weeks. Now
that I am back of the lines taking
a rest after being in combat for
21 days straight I can relax and
catch up on my letters. I am
sitting by a nice hot wood stove
enjoying the comforts of life by
being warm and dry. The weather
is rough and it is snowing
outside. I really feel for the boys
on the front lines as I know
what they are suffering. I certainly
had some experiences in the past
three weeks that I will long
remember the rest of my days. Of
course I expect to be back at
the front in another two weeks

Letter: Nov. 10, 1944, from Teen to his sister Gladys

Teen on April 24, 1945, just before his regiment
marched on a small series of towns along the Danube River

Teen on left, taken at Bad Ort, Germany,
just after the town was captured

Rupprecht Gerngross speaking into the microphone
that he and his troops seized from Nazi leadership

April 29, 1945, Allied Sherman tanks move
into Munich, Germany, World War II

Ruins of the Reichstag in Berlin, with Soviet airplanes
flying in formation above, May 1945

American Sgt. Arthur
E. Peters reading *Mein
Kampf* while lounging
on a bed that belonged
to Adolf Hitler

Hitler's private residence in Munich,
where Teen found the pistol

Magazine cover, March 1966

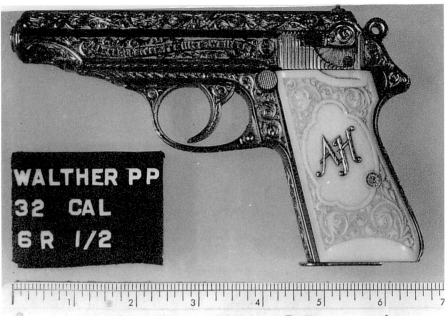

WALTHER PP
32 CAL
6 R 1/2

WICHITA POLICE
LABORATORY

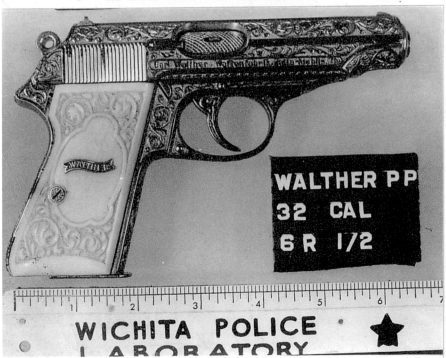

WALTHER PP
32 CAL
6 R 1/2

WICHITA POLICE
LABORATORY

Wichita police photo of gun

WESTERN UNION

1201

A. N. WILLIAMS
PRESIDENT

(13)

The filing time shown in the date line on telegrams and day letters is STANDARD TIME at point of origin. Time of receipt is STANDARD TIME at point of destination

NQ200 42 GOVT=WUX WASHINGTON DC 11 255P

1945 MAY 11 PM 3 22

MRS HELEN R PALM=

40 S EIGHTH AVE

THE SECRETARY OF WAR DESIRES ME TO EXPRESS HIS DEEP REGRET

THAT YOUR HUSBAND 1/LT PALM IRA A WAS SLIGHTLY WOUNDED IN

GERMANY 29 APR 45 CONTINUE TO ADDRESS MAIL TO HIM AS FORMERLY

OR UNTIL NEW ADDRESS IS RECEIVED FROM HIM=

J A ULIO THE ADJUTANT GENERAL.

1/LT 29 45.

THE COMPANY WILL APPRE

Western Union telegram,
May 11, 1945

Helen and Teen Palm, 1943

Lt. Col. Ira A. Palm (Teen) in the late 1950s
while stationed at the Pentagon

June 17, 2006, Joshua's wedding. Left to right Jonathan, Joshua, Susie.

April 2008, Joshua and Daniel at Marine Corps Air Station, New River, NC

At Daniel's OCS graduation, Quantico, VA, July 3, 2010, Joshua, Daniel, and Jonathan

CHAPTER 15

GERNGROSS WAS ON THE RUN. THE FAB WAS SCRAMBLING for cover. The 45th Division was poised to strike Munich. The search for Hitler was in high gear, in the early morning darkness of April 29, 1945; the hunting party was led by Teen Palm.

After the meeting with McNamara, the commanding officers proposed that a small unit of men be sent into Munich with the assistance of FAB members to try to find Hitler. Their target was the German dictator's apartment at 16 Prinzregenten Platz.

Guided by the German soldier who had escorted McNamara from Munich to the Allies, Palm and his band of soldiers traveled by truck, speeding toward the heart of the Nazi Party. They traveled back roads and byways, circling barricades until they could drive no further and stealthily moved through alleys on foot until they were hiding in the darkness across the street from their destination.

It was a four-story building, not at all different from many others in this middle class neighborhood. Nearby were the Osteria Bavaria and Café Heck, restaurants that were longtime Hitler haunts. Hitler had moved into the building in October 1929. It was the third and last of his residences in Munich, the city that, according to Otto Dietrich, his chief of press relations, "was Hitler's chosen home, the city he loved above all others and which he held to be the pearl of Germany." Hugo Bruckman, a publisher dedicated to what he called "the fight for German culture," initially paid the rent. Hitler ceased living there permanently in 1933 and began to split his time between several residences. In 1939, other friends provided the financial help to purchase the entire building for Hitler.

Teen Palm and his men paused to listen and gather their composure. As he had many times before going into battle, Palm withdrew a grimy and creased piece of paper from his pocket. Carefully, he unfolded it. It was almost too dark to see the writing, but that didn't matter. He knew the words to chapter thirty-one, verse eight from the book of Deuteronomy —his war verse— by heart:

> And the LORD, he it is that doth go before thee; he
> will be with thee, he will not fail thee, neither forsake
> thee: fear not, neither be dismayed.

His men waited for Palm to give them a signal. They trusted him with their lives; he had proved his mettle time and again in battle. They had seen how he cared about his soldiers — not only physically but spiritually. And they all believed that not only would he protect them as best he could, but that Teen Palm was ready to die for them.

With a nod of his head, Palm led the men across the street, where they pressed against the side of the building on both sides of the front door. Slowly, Palm pushed on the door. It was unlocked and swung open without a sound.

With Palm leading, the men passed through in single file

and began climbing the two flights of stairs leading to Hitler's apartment.

The nine-room apartment spread over three thousand two hundred square feet of living space. It was in one of those rooms that Hitler's half-niece, Angela "Geli" Raubal, was found dead in September 1931. The young woman, twenty years Hitler's junior and undoubtedly his mistress, had been shot in the chest, and one of Hitler's many guns was found at her side. Terrified of a scandal, Hitler's staff quickly stepped in to officially rule the death a suicide.

The building was silent. None of Palm's men spoke. They knew their job, and they likely had a vision of Hitler's face before them as they crept upward — moments from coming face-to-face with the scourge of the world. *Would there be armed bodyguards with fingers poised on the triggers?* After surviving vicious battles in woods, valleys, and towns over days, weeks, and months, this could be the day they would die.

In what seemed like minutes, but was only seconds, they were outside the door of the apartment. Palm took a moment to scan the men's faces and then, with a violent lunge, he kicked in the door. It sounded like a bomb had been detonated, and Palm, followed by his men, rifles in hand, burst inside.

Quickly, they fanned out in a room-to-room search, scanning the furniture and walls with their flashlights. In the hallway were cupboards holding crystal and china, a rubber plant and a black plaster eagle with folded wings. They found a bedroom decorated with chintz and a bed covered in matching material. There was a large cream-colored safe in the corner, and a plaster cast of Hitler's hands on the table. On a table in the living room was a King George VI mug that, if any of the men had had the time to lift it up, would have played the British national anthem. It had been a gift to Hitler from Chamberlain.

It was immediately apparent that no one was in the apartment. Wherever Hitler was, he was not at 16 Prinzregenten Platz. The place was pristine — as if housecleaners had just finished tidying up after a visit by the Fuehrer.

Palm found himself alone in Hitler's office. He surveyed the room and then walked behind Hitler's rectangular oak desk. He slid back the brown leather chair and saw drawers on each side. He pulled open the top drawer on the right side. There, resting as innocuously as a fountain pen or a letter opener, was a pistol.

It was no ordinary pistol. It was the golden pistol the Walther family gave Hitler nearly six years ago to the day on the dictator's fiftieth birthday. Palm could not decipher the German words that stretched along the barrel. He picked it up and, just as quickly as he had entered the room, stuffed it inside his shirt along with a stack of stationery that had been sitting atop the desk.

Of all of the gifts Hitler received on his fiftieth birthday, this pistol was one of his most prized possessions, and it walked out the door under the shirt of First Lieutenant Teen Palm.

"Let's get out of here," he whispered to his men. "We have to get out of this city now."

As quietly as they had entered, the men crept down the stairs. Seeing the street still deserted, they left and began to retrace their steps. They emerged safely from the city and headed for the Allied front.

Shortly after 7:00 a.m., as they trudged through a thatch of woods, twigs snapping and leaves rustling, a burst of machine-gun fire erupted and then stopped. They hit the ground and scrambled for cover. They hugged the ground and waited in silence. Perhaps the shots weren't meant for them?

After several minutes, Palm and his men began moving forward again, at first on their hands and knees, and then they stood and walked steadily — right into a deadly firefight.

Bullets whizzed and smacked into trees. Mortar shells exploded. Palm took cover and fired in the direction he believed the shots were coming from. And then it happened. With a smack and a sharp sting, a piece of shrapnel pierced his upper left arm. He rolled to the ground, grabbing his sleeve. He felt the warmth of his own blood oozing between his fingers.

Palm took a deep breath and tried to remain calm. He began to mouth his war verse. "He will not fail thee, neither forsake thee: fear not, neither be dismayed."

He prayed that he would not go into shock. He prayed that he would not bleed to death. He prayed that he would get back to the safety of the Allied front.

The gun battle raged for nearly thirty minutes before, almost as if by divine intervention, it stopped. Whoever was shooting at them drifted away. Perhaps they all were killed. Perhaps they feared they were outnumbered and retreated to fight another day.

After several minutes of silence, Palm began calling to his men to regroup and get ready to move out. Some of them did not — could not — reply. They were dead.

Within an hour, the survivors had rejoined their company. Palm's report that Hitler was not at the apartment provided even more credence to the suspicion that he was already in the National Redoubt. Palm was taken to a hospital. For now, his war was over.

The 45th, 42nd, and 3rd Infantry divisions of the Seventh

Army steamrolled into Munich. Though Hitler appeared to have escaped, another of the Axis leaders had not. Two days earlier, a group of Italian partisans had caught up with dictator Benito Mussolini and his mistress, Clara Petacci, near Lake Como. The couple was attempting to flee Italy by traveling with retreating German soldiers.

Their captors took them to the village of Guilino de Mezzegra where Mussolini and Petacci were fatally shot. After that, fifteen members of the group of Italians traveling with them were rounded up and executed.

On April 29, as dawn was breaking and Palm was leaving Munich, the bodies of Mussolini, Petacci, and the others were arriving in Milan, the birthplace of Italian Fascism. Moments after the corpses were dumped onto the Piazzale Loreto, a crowd gathered and began shouting and attempting to mutilate the bodies. Some urinated on the corpses. Photographs were taken and sent worldwide to prove the hated despot was dead.

Then, the bodies of Mussolini and Petacci and two others were hoisted up on an iron bar. They dangled by their heels with pieces of paper bearing their names attached to their feet. A few hours later, Achille Starace, former secretary general of the Fascist Party, was hauled into the square, propped up against a wall, and shot in the back. Then his body was raised on the beam to dangle with the others.

German resistance to the Allies when they reached Munich was largely insignificant. Though at least one-third of the city's buildings were damaged or in ruins — in the previous two years, Allied planes dropped bombs more than five dozen times — Gerngross achieved his hope of saving Munich from complete destruction.

The 179th Regiment established its headquarters in Hitler's

apartment. *Life* magazine would later print a photograph of a soldier lying on Hitler's couch, his boots propped up on the cushions, a copy of Hitler's *Mein Kampf* in his hands. The caption read in part, "The evil dreams which had haunted this room had driven Germany to destitution and destruction ..." Though orders were to not touch any of the items in the apartment, many of the soldiers going in and out could not resist the temptation to take "souvenirs," including the many items emblazoned with "AH" and several other guns that Hitler kept there. These things would later help fuel what would become a lively and lucrative market for Hitler memorabilia.

On the afternoon of April 29, the end finally came for Adolf Hitler. With Russian troops less than a half mile from his bunker located beneath the New Reich Chancellery in Berlin, Hitler and Eva Braun, his longtime mistress, whom he had married a day earlier, went into his study and committed suicide. She swallowed cyanide. Hitler shot himself in the head with a pistol.

On May 1, Eisenhower sent a message to his troops: "To every member of the Allied Expeditionary Force: The whole AEF congratulates the Seventh Army on the Seizure of Munich, the cradle of the Nazi beast."

Six days later, in the early morning hours of May 7, General Alfred Jodl, chief of staff of the German Armed Forces High Command, signed the unconditional surrender of all German forces to the Allies effective May 8.

The ink was barely dry when, in the town of Berchtesgaden, about ninety miles southeast of Munich, Paul Giesler committed suicide.

CHAPTER 16

ON MAY 3, TEEN WROTE TO HELEN TO TELL HER THAT HE
had been wounded:

> *I am in a hospital taking it easy with only a slight shrapnel*
> *wound in the shoulder, so don't worry. I was hit at 7:30 a.m.*
> *in the Battle for Munich.*
>
> *All is well and I'll be as good as new in two weeks. Maybe*
> *the war will be over by then, I hope ... I am thankful to*
> *the Lord for letting me get out so light as others weren't as*
> *fortunate.... I am truly thankful to the Lord for sparing me*
> *and for all His wonderful blessings.*
>
> *I'm awaiting a plane to go to France somewhere and rest*
> *up. I look for a homecoming soon.*
>
> *All my love and kisses*

Teen fully appreciated how blessed he was. He was only
feet away when two of his commanders — John Rahill and
William Robertson — were killed. He had seen many other
members of Company B and the 179th Regiment fall to enemy
fire.

Beginning with the invasion of Sicily in June 1943, and
stretching up to the fall of Munich, the 179th Regiment lost

fifty-five officers and one thousand thirty-six enlisted men in battle. An additional one thousand sixty-two officers and enlisted men were missing or taken prisoner. Teen was among the more than four thousand members of the 179th who were wounded.

The 45th Division, which included the 179th and two other regiments, lost more than seven thousand two hundred killed or missing in action. More than fifty-five thousand were wounded and injured. Palm was also among more than three hundred men from the 179th Regiment awarded the Silver Star and among nearly seven hundred men from the regiment who received a Bronze Star.

But his concern was not with medals and citations. Weighing heavily on his mind was the war in the Pacific and the question of whether he would be sent to fight the Japanese. He wrote to his parents:

I am praising God for seeing me through this war over here and give thanks that it's all over ... The Lord has been merciful and protecting of me all the way and I praise him with all my heart ... He has spared my life a thousand fold. I have a lot to tell you when I get home. I also hope that I will not have to go Pacific bound, but that I can train troops in the states for that campaign. I feel sure that I will be home in a few months for a 30-day leave and then maybe off to the Pacific.

By May 18, he was ready to return to Munich. After several days of riding in boxcars and waiting in train depots, Palm was reunited with Company B in Munich in late May. Along the way, he visited the city of Worms and saw that the giant monument dedicated to Martin Luther was still standing. But the city itself, he wrote to Helen, was nearly destroyed:

You would never recognize it as it's all flat from the war with few buildings left standing. Most of the historical places have also been destroyed. The last time I saw this place was when I crossed the Rhine about 800 yards north of the city and at that time, it was a blazing inferno. The only thing that is still in good condition is the monument to Martin Luther . . . There are about 15,000 people living here now, compared to about 50,000 before the war.

When he arrived in Munich, he found waiting fifty letters from Helen as well as six packages of food, including canned lobster, turkey, and salmon. After existing almost exclusively on K rations for months on the frontline (and losing nearly forty pounds), even canned fish seemed to him a feast.

Palm also confronted one of the worst horrors of the war: Dachau. Upon his return to Munich, he was part of a guard detail from the 179th that was sent to the concentration camp where thousands of men and women too weak to leave were still being tended to by medical personnel.

Palm had missed the Allies' discovery of the camp about ten miles north of Munich because units of the 45th and 42nd divisions came upon the camp the same day he was wounded. Palm was deeply moved by the camp, despite all the cruelties and loss of life he had seen in battle. He wrote to his father:

Here are some pictures of a concentration camp that my company captured and took over for a while. The pictures are self-explanatory and were taken by me so they are not propaganda. These people were dying at the rate of about 70 per day until our medics were able to get the place under control. These people died of hunger and disease. The odor was so bad gas masks had to be worn when burying

these people. It was a horrible place of torture and we even
found some boxcars full of bodies some of which died from
suffocation. These SS troops were the cause of it all and sure
were bad customers.

In June 1945, Palm was assigned to a heavy training schedule designed to prepare him and other troops for warfare in the Pacific. In his letters to Helen, he expressed his hope that the war with Japan would end before he could be sent to fight again.

He got his wish shortly, following the dropping of nuclear bombs on Hiroshima on August 6 and Nagasaki on August 9. The devastation of those two attacks — estimates put the dead at more than two hundred thousand — prompted Japan to announce its surrender on August 15, assuring that Teen's brother, Cliff, would also be heading home.

Palm returned to the States in September, boarding the *Aquitania*, a British cruise ship that had been pressed into service during the war. With hundreds of other soldiers who could now proudly call themselves veterans, Palm sailed back across the Atlantic. He had been gone for sixteen months, but before leaving he had spent his last weeks in France assigned to a military-intelligence school. This would be a defining period for him.

Several times during his service, he had promised in his letters to Helen and his parents that he would have many stories to tell about his days in battle. He had promised himself to do that. But he would discover, as most veterans did, that any desire to share war stories faded the instant their feet landed safely on U.S. soil. It seems likely that Palm's experience in the military-intelligence school and its emphasis on secrecy might have further compelled him to keep a more closed mouth about his exploits, particularly the assault on Hitler's apartment. Perhaps he found it uncomfortable to recount the bloody battles and horror of war — those were memories better set aside. There would be pain in the retelling.

And there was so much to look forward to. It was time to live and not remember, to move forward and not backward, to enjoy the life of promise and love with Helen that they had so long desired.

Whatever the complex reasons, Palm, like many veterans who fought in World War II, rarely spent time reminiscing about his experiences — the battles, the vast destruction of cities and towns, and the enormous and sometimes extraordinarily painful loss of life. But he did confide in the one person who had been instrumental in his spiritual rebirth. That man was his spiritual mentor, Charles Woodbridge.

CHAPTER 17

HIS SHOULDER ACHED AND HE WORE A SLING FROM TIME TO time to ease the pain, but that was a minor irritation compared to the joy Palm felt about being home with Helen. After so many months of being able to express their hopes and dreams and love with only pen and paper, they felt like newlyweds all over again.

Gone were the days when Teen would have to push off to crawl through deep woods and meadows, or to cross a river at night, not knowing if German gun fire was about to erupt. He would no longer have to listen for incoming shells and watch devastating blasts shatter tree trunks and branches, turning them into a fusillade of deadly wooden missiles.

Discharged from the Army, Teen found work with the Veterans Administration, and he happily plunged back into life at First Presbyterian Church of Salisbury. Teen wanted more time to study the Bible. He needed to catch up with Helen's knowledge of Scripture that she gained under Charles Woodbridge's tutelage while Teen was at war. But while those early months back in Salisbury were blissful, Teen knew something was missing — Dr. Charles Woodbridge, the man who had marked his life indelibly.

Several months earlier, as Americans anxiously prayed for

the end of the war, and as Teen prepared to cross the Rhine River, Dr. Samuel M. Glasgow, pastor of the Independent Presbyterian Church in Savannah, Georgia, had sent an invitation to Charles Woodbridge in Salisbury to come and preach.

Woodbridge knew Glasgow well. In 1926, Woodbridge served as a summer assistant to Glasgow, who was a pastor in Knoxville, Tennessee. After Woodbridge went to Salisbury, their paths crossed again in 1938, when Glasgow, who had become pastor of Independent Presbyterian, invited Woodbridge to be a guest preacher. He had made a very favorable impression on the congregation, and he was pleased to be invited back once more for a week.

In March 1945, Woodbridge packed a suitcase and got behind the wheel of his dark green Dodge. Leisurely, he drove the three hundred some miles south to Savannah, through the lush and scenic countryside near Augusta, Georgia. Normally, the Masters Golf Tournament was in full swing at that time, but it had been suspended since 1942 because of the war and groundskeepers were raising turkeys and cattle on the grounds to support the war effort.

Despite his earlier years in the North, Woodbridge was more at home in the South. His parents were Southerners and with each passing year in Salisbury, he felt he was recovering his family's Southern roots. And now he was going to preach in one of the South's more storied cities and in one of its most illustrious churches.

As he made his way into Savannah, Woodbridge was struck by the city's beauty. He had always had a fondness for spring when the azaleas and rhododendron transformed the city into a verdant garden.

While Woodbridge was in Savannah, Glasgow treated him like royalty, and the congregation warmly received his messages. Shortly after Woodbridge returned to Salisbury, he received yet another invitation. Glasgow had announced he was resigning the pastorate of Independent Presbyterian, and the church elders invited Woodbridge to become the next pastor. A seemingly innocent request to have him spend a week there may well have been Glasgow's way of introducing Woodbridge to the congregants in the hope they would see him as a natural successor.

It was a hard decision to make. After eight years in Salisbury, Woodbridge had come to dearly cherish his ministry there. And he loved his parishioners, particularly Helen and Teen Palm. For more than a year, Helen had worked closely with him as his secretary. He was praying for Teen's safe return from the war and eagerly anticipated hearing about his combat experiences and how his spiritual life had weathered the war.

But after much thought and prayer, Woodbridge agreed to take over the pulpit in Savannah. It seemed a natural break. He was about to receive his doctorate in church history from Duke University. His family had expanded to four children (their three daughters had been joined by a son, John, born in 1941) and a move to a larger church would be financially beneficial.

Soon after completing his degree at Duke in June 1945, Woodbridge, with a mixture of sadness and excitement, bid farewell to Salisbury. His wife Ruth found it particularly difficult to say good-bye to Helen Palm; the two were soul mates. They promised each other that they would write regularly and visit as frequently as possible.

As beautiful as Savannah was in full bloom, this was a city that had fallen on hard times. Its economy had slackened considerably during the 1930s, spared none of the Depression's woes. Many of its parks were overgrown and untended. Dilapidated buildings lined the cobblestone River Street. The city's wharf and an ever-increasing number of its once-grand mansions were in a sorry state of disrepair.

Lady Nancy Astor, a Virginian by birth who had been the first woman to be seated in England's House of Commons, visited Savannah around this time and famously referred to the city as looking like a "pretty woman with a dirty face."

Nonetheless, during the war, the economy had received a boost from the military ship-building industry in Savannah's port and the city was beginning to show some signs of recovering its splendor. Its premier eating haunts — Pirates' House at East Broad and Bay Street and the Olde Pink House at 23 Abercorn Street — were thriving. Oak trees shrouded in Spanish moss lined Savannah's streets, converting them into picturesque marvels. Neighborhoods rang with the sounds of clanging bells from the trolleys that rolled down cobblestone streets.

Savannah boosters printed brochures portraying the city's economic future as promising while it continued to embrace a long, noble, historic past filled with romance and sentiment. The population in metropolitan Savannah had reached 117,970 in 1940 and would grow to 162,000 by the end of the decade.

The Woodbridges' new home was the church manse at 101 East Washington Avenue, and what a home it was: stately, well-preserved, and a spacious two stories. Savannah life was pleasurable for the Woodbridge family. Charles immersed himself in the church and hoped he could forge the same lasting and enriching relationships that he had enjoyed in Salisbury. The children were busy with school, and Ruth began getting involved in social and charitable organizations. They were well cared for by Emma, the maid and cook provided by the church.

Young John spent most days playing fetch with his dog, Skippy. It wouldn't be long before he would be heading off to school like his older sisters. Savannah in the 1940s was a place where even six-year-olds walked to school if they lived close enough, and the Woodbridge family lived just three blocks from the Charles Ellis Elementary School.

If John arose early enough and was in the backyard, he would see the "divers," as his father called them, scavenging through the family's trash containers lined up beside the garage in the alley. He gave it little thought as scavenging was a regular sight, and he regarded it as something only poor people did.

A curious boy, John spent hours exploring the neighborhood for fallen bird nests, lost pennies, or a good tree to climb. He liked to stand on Habersham Street to watch the trolleys, bells clanging, rumble down the center of the cobblestone way. He loved to ride Savannah's trolleys but did not do so very often. His parents usually drove to family or social engagements in the new Buick the church had presented to the family upon their arrival.

One of his favorite games was playing marbles in the sand with neighborhood boys. The ultimate treat was to go to a friend's home, flop on the family rug, and listen to the *Sky King* radio show with cookies and milk. He regularly persuaded his father to give him a quarter to send off for the latest Sky King decoder ring with a secret compartment.

His father doted on him — buying him a pony named Moonbeam that was kept on a friend's farm. He took John crabbing on the seashore, and together they raised baby chicks into hens in a coop behind their home. His father was a hero to him.

It was an idyllic life for a young child. He was well taken care of by his mother, father, and sisters Norma, Rosemary, and Pat. He adored Emma, a good-hearted, generous woman. Indeed, Emma played a large role in raising the children because their parents were so deeply involved in church life. Emma did not find it a nuisance that John collected snails, fed them bits of lettuce, and housed them in a cardboard box in the kitchen — even though nearly every morning would find one or two of the small critters absent from the box. It was easy enough to track the escapees by the sticky trails they left behind.

By the fall of 1946, when Teen and Helen were reunited and settled in Salisbury, the Woodbridges began urging them to relocate to Savannah. They urged them to visit and offered to help Teen find a job there.

"We miss you both more than I can possibly tell you," Charles wrote in a letter to Teen and Helen. "I am still going to hope that you may be able to settle in Savannah. This is a lovely city and I know you would be happy here."

In December, Charles invited the couple to spend the Christmas holidays with his family. He suggested Teen could use the time to make some contacts for a potential job "in the hope that perhaps the Lord might lead you both here. I have already spoken to one or two leading businessmen about you."

Teen and Helen made the trip, and Teen did request a transfer to the Veterans Administration in Savannah. When he was turned down, he sent an application to the Army for a commission — to return as an officer with an eye toward a career and advancement in rank.

When no response was forthcoming, he put it aside in his

mind until the day the telegram arrived, offering him a commission in the Army with orders to report to Fort Benning, Georgia. Helen and Teen were torn. They had come to believe he was finished with Army life. Now, Teen wondered if it was the Lord's plan to use them as missionaries in the military.

They made a hurried visit to the chaplain at Fort Bragg to seek counsel. He advised that officers who were too severe in their religious convictions would not find acceptance among other officers.

They also visited Savannah and Teen brought a special gift for Charles Woodbridge: Hitler's pistol. He wanted to give the gold-plated firearm, which represented a night of bravery, as a special souvenir, a token of love and gratitude, to a man of peace, a man of God, the man who introduced him to Christ.

There is no record of what was said during that visit or how Teen decided to give the gun and the personalized stationery he had taken from Hitler's Munich apartment to Woodbridge. He respected and loved Charles as a spiritual teacher and friend and even more, he considered him like a brother. And Woodbridge treated Teen as a brother as well.

Perhaps he was simply motivated by respect and love for his dear friend, the man who had brought him the knowledge of Jesus Christ and who had, in essence, given him the spiritual tools to survive the horrors of war and to meet its dark duties with great courage.

Woodbridge was honored by the gift and its significance — not only because it had belonged to Hitler, but because Teen took it in the course of risking his life for his country. Teen was, in Woodbridge's view, a genuine war hero.

Teen and Helen returned to Salisbury, reluctantly rejecting entreaties from Woodbridge and his wife to move to Savannah. In January 1947, Woodbridge wrote to them to express his family's sadness at their decision to remain in Salisbury and to thank Teen for the pistol:

Needless to say, we are greatly disappointed. But of course, as usual, we must yield our regrets to the Lord. Perhaps one of these days He may work it out in a way far better than our feeble planning!

But in the meantime, come see us whenever you can find an excuse, or whenever you cannot, for that matter! It's only 300 miles and what's that among friends in the Lord.

Thank you so much for information concerning the pistol. I am delighted to have both — pistol and information.

The work here continues to move forward nicely. We all send you both our love. See you soon, I hope.

As ever your friend in Christ

Woodbridge was immensely proud of the pistol. In a letter to the Palms, Ruth Woodbridge wrote that he was showing the pistol to "everyone" who came to their home. She said he loved telling the dramatic story of how Teen broke into Hitler's apartment and left with the pistol and stationery.

Woodbridge showed it to his church members. He showed it to visiting missionaries and speakers who visited the church. And he showed it to his children.

John was not yet seven years old when, one evening, his father summoned him to his second-floor office. As he slowly walked up the stairs, John wondered if he had done something deserving a reprimand. His curiosity rose when nothing came to mind.

As he stepped through the doorway into the dimly lit room, he saw his father seated at the wooden desk where he worked on his weekly sermons. A lamp cast an amber glow on the green writing pad in the center of the desk.

"Ah, John," he said, turning in his chair. "Come into my study. I want to show you something."

John edged closer to the desk. His father reached into a drawer on the right side of the desk and pulled out sheets of stationery. He reached once more into the drawer and withdrew an object.

John's eyes widened.

It was a gun!

"This gun belonged to Adolf Hitler," his father said, looking him directly in the eye.

Cautiously, John looked at the stationery. He had heard the name Hitler before, and he knew that Hitler had started a terrible war. The name "Adolf Hitler" was printed in gold letters across the top of the stationery. The letters almost jumped off the paper.

John said nothing.

His father held the pistol in his right hand. John had never been close up to any pistol before, let alone one that had belonged to Adolf Hitler.

The gold gun was tarnished, and there appeared to be a dark crust along the pearl grips. "Did that really come from Hitler?" John asked.

"Yes, it did, John," Woodbridge said. "Teen Palm gave me this stationery and he gave me this pistol."

"But where did he get it?" John persisted.

"When Teen was in the war, he was sent to find Hitler," Woodbridge said. "He told me he was the first soldier to come through the door of Hitler's apartment in Munich."

"Was Hitler there?" John asked.

"No, he wasn't, John," Woodbridge said. "Fortunately, the

apartment was empty. Teen was the first person inside, and he didn't have much time, so he went to Hitler's desk. When he opened the desk drawers, he found this pistol and that stationery."

John could only nod his head. His eyes were glued to the pistol.

Finally, he looked up at his father. "Was he a hero?"

Woodbridge smiled. "Yes, son, Teen was a genuine hero. He was awarded medals for his heroism in the war. But he doesn't like to talk about it — especially with children. So, please, son, I ask you not to talk to him about this when you see him."

And so, obedient child that John was, he never did.

CHAPTER 18

AFTER MUCH SOUL-SEARCHING, TEEN ACCEPTED THE ARMY'S offer of a commission and reported for the Advanced Infantry Officers' course at Fort Benning, Georgia. He believed that the Army would be his lifework and provide him an opportunity to be a witness for Christ among soldiers. On March 28, 1947, Teen reported for duty and wrote his sister, Gladys:

> Arrived at Fort Benning today and the way things look I'll be here about a year. I have been attached to the student training regiment, handling Officer Candidate School men like I was in 1942.
>
> The Army is not the same — there isn't much activity of troops like before. Seems strange to be in uniform, especially away from Helen.
>
> I am in the field with troops from 7:00 a.m. to 5:30 p.m. each day and it takes a lot out of me right now. The heat bothers me a little but I guess I'll get in shape sometime in the future. I may very well end up a 30-year man.

Helen soon moved to join Teen. The relocation provided more opportunities to visit the Woodbridge family in Savannah. The Woodbridge children enjoyed Helen and Teen's visits. Teen frequently spent time with them and was genuinely interested in hearing about their lives. Rosemary thought Teen in uniform was "the handsomest man" she had ever seen, and sister Norma was struck by how closely he seemed to listen to what the children had to say. He was also spontaneous, offering an impromptu clarinet lesson to Patsy one moment, launching into a popular song the next.

The families grew closer, drawn together as much by their friendship as by their deep and abiding faith in God. On July 13, 1947, to the Woodbridges' delight, Teen and Helen became members of Charles's church. Teen spoke to the congregation, giving his "testimony" about how he had come to find faith in Christ. The moment was broadcast to thousands of people in southern Georgia and northern Florida who listened weekly on radio station WCCP.

The following week, Ruth wrote to Helen and noted that many in the congregation were still talking about Teen's speech. Ruth said that at the end of the month, the family planned to head to Camp of the Woods in Speculator, New York, for a vacation. It was a Christian resort and conference center, and one of their favorite vacation spots. Norma Jean, the oldest daughter, was already there, spending her summer as a member of the camp staff. Charles had been on the staff as a youth years earlier.

On July 25, 1947, Charles wrote to Helen and Teen and mentioned Hitler's pistol. Charles had been trying to make sense of what appeared to be an inscription in German on the side of the pistol and had previously written to Teen, asking for his help. The task was difficult because the gun was tarnished and a dark residue covered parts of its sides and grips.

A few days later, the Woodbridge family shuttered its home and drove to Camp of the Woods, where Charles sometimes served as a guest speaker. They stayed in a tent and spent much of their time meeting new friends and renewing old relationships. They attended Bible classes and evening concerts. They swam and canoed in Lake Pleasant.

Seemingly in an instant, it was time to pack up and drive back to Savannah. The trip was more than a thousand miles, and by the time they drew under the portico of their home, they were exhausted. The weather was typical for a Savannah summer: hot and sultry. It was so uncomfortable that Charles and Ruth even allowed the girls to wear shorts — clothing they had long considered inappropriate for young women.

Charles unlocked the side door, and all four children bounded into the stuffy home. They stopped in their tracks, though, gawking at their normally pristine living room that was now in a state of disarray. The piano stool stood in a pool of liquid that gave off the unmistakable stench of urine. The piano legs were stained with the liquid as well. Sheet music for Rosemary's violin, and Patsy's music books, left in the piano bench, were ruined.

The children shouted for their parents, and Charles and Ruth came running. They too were taken aback by the sight. It was obvious to them what had happened: one or more intruders had broken into the home.

For a moment, the family stood silently, trying to absorb the disturbing scene. The feeling of being personally violated began churning uneasily inside Charles. As he stood there, he felt a growing sense that something was particularly odd about this burglary, a feeling that was confirmed as he began a room-to-room search and noticed that expensive silver candlesticks and silver candy dishes sitting in plain sight in the dining room were untouched.

He went upstairs to explore the bedrooms. As he entered

his office, nothing seemed amiss. He walked to his desk and pulled open the top right drawer. His heart sank. The drawer was empty. Hitler's pistol was gone.

Hurriedly, Charles finished taking inventory and confirmed his initial inkling. Except for a few articles of his clothing, the only thing taken was his most prized possession: the golden gun and some stationery that one of his closest personal friends had obtained by risking his life.

Charles called the police and two officers arrived shortly. Rosemary later remembered listening from the hallway as her distraught father filled in the policemen who poked around looking for any clues. They discovered that a rear window had pry marks on the sill, suggesting the thief or thieves had entered there. And then the police left. They did not have much hope of solving the crime.

Readers of the *Savannah News* would not have guessed from the paper's brief article about the burglary how deeply upsetting it was for Woodbridge. There was no mention of the pistol. Did Charles tell the police about the missing gun? Was he embarrassed to say that he kept such an object in his home?

Charles bemoaned the loss of the pistol for a time and then moved on with his life.

CHAPTER 19

TEEN PALM FLOURISHED UPON HIS RETURN TO THE ARMY and was promoted to captain. But the promotion paled in comparison to the long-awaited birth of their daughter, Susie, in April of 1948. They had long yearned to have a child — their prayers and hopes had been expressed many times in their letters before and during the war. Susie's birth was the answer to their prayers and the prayers of many friends and family members.

In the late summer, Teen reported to Bamberg, Germany, in the 1st Infantry Division. Helen and Susie stayed behind — the Army did not permit ship travel for infants less than six months old. Teen, a doting and hands-on father, was certain Susie was in the best of hands but knew he would sorely miss his precious daughter until they could be reunited as a family when she was old enough to make the trip.

Germany was far different for Teen than it had been three years earlier when he moved from foxhole to foxhole and braved enemy fire.

After the war, Germany was divided into four zones, each controlled by one of the Allies — the United States, Britain, France, and the Soviet Union — each with its own military government until a national government could be established and the country reunited.

Although Berlin, the largest city in Germany, was situated wholly in the Soviet zone of influence, the city also had been divided into four zones, each controlled by one of the Allies. Over time, the three zones controlled by the Western Allies came to be known as West Berlin, and the zone controlled by the Soviets became known as East Berlin.

In the post-war years, the Soviet Union began to dominate Eastern Europe, occupying or asserting controlling influence over Poland, Czechoslovakia, Hungary, Romania, and Bulgaria. It was the beginning of the Cold War.

In 1946, Winston Churchill, no longer prime minister of England, traveled to Westminster College in Fulton, Missouri, where he told a gathering of some forty thousand, "From Stettin in the Baltic to Trieste in the Adriatic an iron curtain has descended across the Continent. Behind that line lie all the capitals of the ancient states of Central and Eastern Europe — Warsaw, Berlin, Prague, Vienna, Budapest, Belgrade, Bucharest, and Sofia. All these famous cities and the populations around them lie in what I must call the Soviet sphere, and all are subject, in one form or another, not only to Soviet influence but to a very high and in some cases increasing measure of control from Moscow."

"Iron Curtain" became a shorthand term to describe the massive walls and fences that divided the Eastern bloc countries from Western Europe. In an attempt to create some stability, the United States and Britain combined their zones of Germany into one, called Bizonia. (In 1949, when France joined, it would become Trizonia).

In response, in 1948, the Soviets mandated searches of all Western convoys traveling through East Germany. It was an attempt to push the West out of Berlin. France, the United States, and Britain refused to allow the searches.

The Soviets then cut all land-based traffic to West Berlin on June 27, 1948, halting all truck and rail shipments. The response was the Berlin Airlift — more than 270,000 flights hauling more than two million tons of food and supplies. The airlift ended in May 1949 when the Soviets lifted the blockade. By that time, Berlin stood as a clear symbol of the rift between the United States and the Soviet Union.

Shortly before the airlift ended, Helen joined Teen with eleven-month-old Susie, and once again, the family was together.

Palm immersed himself in his expanded duties as a captain, but also made time for his Christian mission. In Bamberg, he started teaching an adult Sunday school class, beginning a life-long pursuit to provide not only for the physical needs and training of his men, but for their spiritual welfare too.

To some observers, that may have seemed paradoxical. He was a member of the world's greatest fighting machine, yet he preached faith in the Prince of Peace. Long before, however, Palm had reconciled that seeming contradiction, concluding from his reading of the Bible that God often uses force to combat evil.

"When evil nations attempt to overrun the world," he once wrote, "and destroy freedom to worship God, God uses Christians to go to battle and destroy these forces in order that his Word may still be proclaimed. The Lord commanded Christians to be a witness unto him to the uttermost parts of the earth. I am thankful that being in the Army I have an opportunity to have a part in this great commission and I want to use the rest of my life, insignificant as it is, to his glory."

Palm knew deep in his heart that he would have been lost

long ago without the gift of faith. Just as Charles Woodbridge had opened his heart and mind years earlier, so Palm sought to provide an opportunity for the men and women in the military to find their way to Christ.

His military superiors found Palm to be extremely conscientious and diligent. Further, he cared deeply for the men under his command. Those men believed him fair, honest, and direct. In response, they worked hard to please him.

His efforts paid off. Palm was promoted to the rank of major in January 1949, and was awarded the silver leaves of a lieutenant colonel in December 1950. And wherever he was sent, he and Helen worked as a team, viewing each assignment to a new location as an assignment from God to share the gospel. They usually first became friends and supporters of the post chaplain and volunteered to teach Sunday school classes and minister where needed. Helen always established a midweek daytime women's Bible study class and often taught vacation Bible school for children in the summers. They attended weekly evening Bible studies as well as retreats. They truly considered themselves to be missionaries to the military. As Teen's rank ascended, they were advised to do certain things to enhance his career, such as attending particular parties or joining the women's club, but they demurred, remaining focused on their mission. Teen continued to advance anyway.

Palm's extraordinary potential earned him a transfer in 1951 to Fort Leavenworth, Kansas, to attend the Command and General Staff College. There, Palm not only taught Sunday school, but also preached sermons at the Leavenworth penitentiary and filled in as guest pastor at a local church, delivering sermons based on Scripture he selected and painstakingly wrote out in capital letters on ruled paper.

Frequently, he preached a sermon to the officers about

what it meant to be a true Christian believer and the differ-ence between life on Earth and life with God after death.

"Those of us who have felt the sting of battle have seen the instinctive methods used to preserve physical life," he would say. "Self-preservation in all walks of life is a natural impulse, which automatically reacts to fight for the last breath of physi-cal life. But this natural life, important as it is, lasts for only a few score of years only to end and return to the dust from whence it came."

He was fond of quoting James 4:14: "Whereas ye know not what shall be on the morrow. For what is your life? It is even a vapour, that appeareth for a little time, and then vanisheth away."

In one sermon, Palm addressed the command officers directly:

"You may make decisions that move platoons, battalions, divisions or even Armies. You may make a decision that turns the whole course of global war to victory. But the greatest decision you ever make in your life — the one that plots your eternal destination — is the road upon which you choose to travel. Someday you will have to answer the question: What have I done with Jesus?"

During these years, the Palms also became involved in the Officers' Christian Union, an interdenominational fellowship of Christians who sought to grow in their faith and share it with their fellow officers.

In 1952, Teen, Helen, and Susie moved to Fort Monroe, Virginia, for a three-year tour of duty. It was a time they con-sidered their most spiritually fruitful and rich. Three years later, in 1955, they drove to Monterey, California, where Helen and Susie settled in among students at the Navy War College while Teen went on an "unaccompanied tour" in Korea, two years after the armistice was signed to end the war there. Helen and Susie saw him off and would not see him again until his return eighteen months later. As they did during the war, Helen and Teen faithfully wrote letters back and forth nearly every day.

In Korea, Teen's battalion was situated about four miles from regimental headquarters near the village of Tongori. When he arrived, there was no chaplain, and the chapel was a rundown shack. Palm arranged for a chaplain to be transferred to the unit, and he helped his men build a chapel. Soon it was overflowing with men and women for church services, Bible studies, and Sunday school classes.

While in Monterey, Helen continued attending weekly Officers' Christian Union Bible studies and taught Sunday school. At the same time, Palm and another Christian officer, King Coffman, were instrumental in helping Korean officers start the Korean Officers' Christian Union.

Teen returned from Korea by ship, arriving in San Francisco where he and Helen and Susie were joyfully reunited. They drove cross-country to their new home in Arlington, Virginia, where Teen had accepted a new assignment at the Pentagon. Teen passed the time on the long haul by making flash cards so Susie could master the multiplication tables.

Promoted to colonel, Palm was named commanding officer of the 1st Battle Group in Augsburg, Germany, so the family moved once again. They resumed their ministry in Germany. The Palms arranged a visit by Dr. Woodbridge to speak to high-ranking officers in his command. The Officers' Christian Union convened an international conference at Berchtesgaden's General Walker Hotel, where the weekly meetings were held. Ironically, the hotel was built during Hitler's regime for Air Marshall Hermann Goering's Luftwaffe. After the war, it was taken over by the American forces and used for recreational and religious retreats for the military.

More than three hundred people from nine nations were in attendance. Helen led a Bible study and prayer session for women. One of the teachers was Pastor A. W. Jackson from Cherrydale Baptist Church in Arlington, Virginia, where the Palms had ministered while Teen was at the Pentagon.

Susie would later recall attending meetings where the verses of Psalm 121:1–2 were prominently displayed at the front of the rooms: "I will lift up mine eyes unto the hills, from whence cometh my help. My help cometh from the LORD, which made heaven and earth."

In 1961, Palm and the fifteen hundred men he oversaw were chosen for special duty in Berlin.

Although years had passed since the airlift, Berlin remained a volatile focal point in the continuing tension between the United States and the Soviet Union. East Germans were becoming increasingly impatient with the oppressive politics and failing economies of the Communist regime, so they began fleeing to West Berlin by the hundreds daily.

Frustrated by the talent drain and the clear message being sent by the exodus, the East German government, in the early morning hours of August 13, 1961, closed the border with West Germany. It began erecting what became known as the Berlin Wall — separating families from each other and people from their businesses and jobs.

At first, the East Germans erected a wire fence with barbed-wire entanglements. Streets along the nearly one-hundred-mile fence were ripped up so that people would not attempt to barrel through in vehicles. Concrete blocks and fortifications also were installed. Tanks were stationed along the route, and trains and subways were cut off.

The first Berlin Brigade, as the battle groups assigned to Berlin were called, was summoned in response to the border shutdown. Palm's battle group was ordered to replace that unit on December 7, 1961.

To get into West Berlin, replacement troops had to be transported in convoys of trucks over a 110-mile section of East German territory. The sudden announcement that fifteen hundred troops would be coming in and fifteen hundred would be leaving at the same time — putting three thousand men on the road in the Communist nation — was perceived as a threat by the Soviets.

Before the first convoy could even depart, East Germany and the Soviet Union began making threats. Free movements of U.S. occupation troops had never been guaranteed, officials of those governments declared. They began threatening to block all traffic going to West Berlin.

Tass, the official Soviet news agency, branded the shuttling of troops a "dangerous act of military display" that was "fraught with dangerous consequences."

The Soviet statements sparked fear that World War III would erupt. Once again, as he had in Munich, Teen Palm would play a key role in leading troops into what could be harm's way.

Six months earlier, President John F. Kennedy had met with Soviet Premier Nikita Khrushchev for a two-day summit to discuss the increasing tension in Berlin. Khrushchev had all but threatened war over Berlin and criticized Kennedy broadly over Cold War issues, including nuclear weapons.

On the final day of the summit, Khrushchev told Kennedy, "It is up to the U.S. to decide whether there will be war or peace." Kennedy replied, "Then, Mr. Chairman, there will be war. It will be a cold winter."

On November 27, less than two weeks before Palm and his unit were assembled on the West German border, Llewellyn Thompson, the U.S. ambassador to Russia, sent a letter to U.S. Secretary of State Dean Rusk outlining what was at stake — and that included war.

The letter said in part that "the Soviets seem convinced that West Germany will obtain atomic arms and doubtless wish to batten down the hatches before this happens. Along the same line, there are doubtless many Soviets who think that 'certain circles' in the United States are bent upon the breakup of the communist empire even at the risk of war." Thompson advised Rusk, "I should think the President should in reply express his shock at Khrushchev's position, state that evidently there is little hope for a broad agreement at this time but that we should at least make every effort to prevent war."

Rusk sent a telegram to the American mission in Berlin on December 1, saying that Kennedy had requested a "prompt evaluation of any new situation arising in Berlin ... Command and other channels are in high state of readiness."

The telegram noted that the official position was that the troop movement was a routine exercise and emphatically pointed out the United States' long-established right to be in Berlin.

The following day, Kennedy sent a letter to Khrushchev. "Western forces are in West Berlin now — and they will remain there as long as the people of West Berlin want them to remain," Kennedy declared. "Western rights of access to West Berlin preceded and are independent of the Soviet Union's creation of the present East German regime ... I want to emphasize again that what best serves peace, not merely prestige, must be our chief yardstick."

When the first convoys left West Germany on December 7,

the eyes of the world were watching. Newspapers across the United States carried front-page stories with headlines saying, "Convoy Defies Reds" and "U.S. Battle Units Start Crossing East Germany." In article after newspaper article, Teen Palm was identified as the principal commander of the American battle group destined for Berlin. No one knew whether Palm's unit, outnumbered by Russian and East German forces, would be attacked, overwhelmed, and destroyed.

To the relief of the Allies, the Soviets and East Germans allowed the convoys to pass without incident. Palm and his unit were safely inside West Berlin, and the crisis was over. Palm was later singled out for his leadership during that tense period, not only for the manner in which his men performed, but also for his participation in religious activities that contributed to strengthening the morale of the troops. Brigadier General Frederick O. Hartel wrote a commendation letter to Palm, saying, in part:

> *I was most gratified to see you, one of our major commanders, speak to the community and lead in religious observances. Spiritual leadership is an integral part of command responsibility and must be provided not only to the troops we command, but to the families beside them.*

He was also praised by Major General B. F. Taylor:

> *For a period of three months his Battle Group was absent from this command while on duty in Berlin. The move, by road, occurred in December 1961 while the Berlin Crisis was still hot. Both the move and the assumption of position in Berlin received the highest of praise from all senior command echelons. The continuing top performance, smartness and*

discipline of the troops and the subsequent well organized
departure again was noted by all. I received letters from
General Clarke and General Watson, CG, Berlin, commending
Colonel Palm and his Battle Group on their actions and
attitude in their difficult task. For his demonstrated fine
command leadership and inspiration, Colonel Palm has well
merited these exceptional commendations. Colonel Palm has
put great drive — and realism in the training of his Battle
Group. His high standards, emphasis on a maximum of field
training and his personal interest and emphasis have resulted
in his battle group being in a very high condition of realistic
combat readiness.

Life came full circle for Palm when he returned to the
states with Helen and Susie in 1963. He was assigned to Fort
Meade near Baltimore, the place where he and Helen had bid
farewell, lingering at the bus stop, before he went off to war.

But it turned out to be an unhappy homecoming. While
still in Germany, Palm had begun experiencing pain in his
back that would not be eased. At Fort Meade, he developed
phlebitis in his calf.

After only two months as chief of the Training Division,
Palm was admitted to Kimbrough Army Hospital. Doctors
discovered some enlarged nodes, but the nature of his illness
eluded them.

After nearly three months and repeated batteries of tests, doctors conducted diagnostic surgery and found a growth behind
his pancreas. A biopsy confirmed their worst fears; Teen Palm
had Hodgkin's disease, cancer of the lymphatic system.

For the next two years, Palm bravely and stoically battled
his illness, sometimes spending two or three afternoons a
week at Walter Reed Army Hospital receiving radiation and
chemotherapy treatments.

Susie, barely a teenager then, later recalled it as a difficult time but one of unparalleled unity. "Our closeness as a family was related directly to our closeness to the Lord," she said. "A day never passed that our family didn't have devotions together morning and night."

Though Susie attended a Christian high school out of state, requiring her to be away from home, Teen faithfully wrote weekly letters.

They were as close as a father and daughter could be, despite the frequent moves and the demands of military life. Along the way, Teen taught Susie to play softball, to use a camera, and to know the joy of music, including encouraging her to join the school chorus and take piano lessons.

Despite his cancer treatments, he kept up his daily routine as best he could. He taught Susie how to drive during her summer vacation. He continued to lead Officers' Christian Union meetings. At home, he always dried the dishes after eating, something he had done all his life.

In November 1965, he was hospitalized for abdominal surgery. For the next several weeks, as he recuperated, a stream of friends from civilian life and from the military paraded through his room. Visitors found him sitting erect with his shoulders thrown back. He greeted them the same way every time: "Praise the Lord."

Teen Palm faced his illness as he had faced combat — with an abiding trust in God and a firm belief that life is a journey to the ultimate destination: united with Jesus in heaven.

On one occasion, as he was being prepared for surgery, he told his doctor, "I am going to take a trip."

"That's nice," the doctor said. "Where do you expect to go?"

"To heaven," Palm said.

"That's a good attitude," the doctor said.

"But, Sir," Palm said, flashing his brilliant smile. "That's not an attitude. It's a fact, and I'm looking forward to seeing the Lord Jesus Christ."

Palm had an uncanny ability to speak about God in a manner that was inviting and nonthreatening. Over the years, he had been a powerful witness for Christ. The long days confined to a hospital bed were no exception. Glowing with confidence in his salvation, he lived more for others than for himself. He never faltered or wavered in his beliefs, and now, in his final battle, more than ever, he eagerly sought to spread the Word of God.

His favorite question always was: What is the gospel?

Unfailingly, he wouldn't wait for an answer but would immediately reply with his life verse from Romans 1:16: "Why, 'It is the power of God unto salvation to every one that believeth.'"

In his last letter to Susie, dated March 1, 1966, Teen wrote, "All we can do [is] put our whole trust in Him for all things. Thank the Lord we belong to Him for all eternity and He has saved our souls."

Six months after his surgery, on April 11, 1966, the cancer he had fought so valiantly and that caused him great physical pain finally took his life. He was only fifty-three years old.

Of the many glowing tributes that followed was this from Colonel Arlo W. Mitchell:

When Teen was commissioned in the U.S. Army, he took an oath to support and defend the Constitution of the United States against all enemies, foreign and domestic. I am confident that at the same time, in his heart, he likewise swore to defend his Lord — our Lord — against all enemies. Thus he dedicated his material life to the defense of our country and his spiritual life to the defense of our Lord.

He was never ashamed of his Lord, and neither did he make others ashamed to admit they did not know the Lord. One sensed that he only wanted to help his fellow man find the way. I don't believe he ever tried to change anyone's habits — he simply introduced people to our Savior and he then knew that He would change our ways and solve our problems.

I feel the reason for his tremendous influence on others was that he never judged others — he just wanted to share his joy in the Lord. His life and the way he lived it reflected the shining presence of the Lord.

Colonel Gunnar Hage remembered Palm for his leadership and spirit whether at the Pentagon, in battle, in Bible study, or with his family.

As a younger officer, he was part of what the Army calls the "Queen of Battle," the infantry, and rose to the position of command of his unit. In this position, one is 100 percent responsible for his men — from their equipment, food, clothing, ammunition and housing to their conduct in garrison and actions in the performance of their mission in battle.

This calls for training, experience, courage and leadership. These same qualities were recognized when, as a senior officer, Teen was given key staff positions as well as even greater command assignments of grave responsibility.

Teen was one of the few, one of the special ones, who obviously considered the Lord's will and desire in all things, and moment by moment was about his Father's business.

Two days after he died, Teen Palm was buried in Arlington National Cemetery. It was an overcast, rainy day with temperatures sitting in the forties.

Among those present was Charles Woodbridge. At an emotional church service he spoke about his beloved friend, describing with deep affection the valor, faithfulness, and dedication Teen had embodied during his short life. To honor his friend, Woodbridge dedicated much of his sermon to preaching the life text which they both had shared for many years: "For I am not ashamed of the Gospel of Christ: for it is the power of God unto salvation to every one that believeth."

Then at Arlington National Cemetery, Woodbridge and others accompanied Teen's cortege to his grave, as per military custom, and there he presided over the burial service. Eight months later, Teen Palm was awarded posthumously the Legion of Merit — one of the highest honors conferred by the U.S. Army — for "exceptionally meritorious conduct in the performance of outstanding services."

EPILOGUE

IT IS ANOTHER SNOWY DECEMBER DAY, AND JOHN WOOD-bridge is once again sitting in the family room of his home on the outskirts of Lake Forest, north of Chicago. Five years have passed since the night he sat here and read about the auction of one of Adolf Hitler's firearms in a scroll running at the bottom of a televised news program. His memory jarred that night, he began a journey into his own past. But what started as an attempt to satisfy his curiosity became something else, something much bigger and more meaningful.

"Yes, it was Hitler's pistol that began this journey," Wood-bridge says. "But it turned out that the gun, and my interest in what happened to the gun Teen Palm had given to my father, became secondary to what I did discover about war and hero-ism and faith."

In the more than seventy years since the end of World War II, the attraction of Nazi memorabilia has ebbed and flowed. Thousands of German pistols, ammunition belts, uniforms, and helmets were shipped home by American soldiers. And most of them, not surprisingly, wound up stashed under beds and in footlockers, garages, and attics, where they gathered dust, mostly forgotten — except for items with any link to Adolf Hitler. His personal possessions that have been bought and sold over the years include a desk, a limousine, stationery, and books. Items that once belonged to Hitler's longtime mistress, Eva Braun, have brought spirited bidding. This demand has fueled a lively trade in forgeries. In 1983, the German magazine *Stern* published what it said were the personal diaries of Hitler. They were all fakes.

Who stole Hitler's pistol from Charles Woodbridge's home? Was it someone who had heard Woodbridge talking about his treasure, perhaps a neo-Nazi who saw it as a prize, or an idol to be cherished and held up as a source of power? Right after World War II, a neo-Nazi group called the Columbians sowed racial hatred and bigotry in Georgia.

After disappearing from the Woodbridge home, the pistol Teen Palm took from Hitler's desk first resurfaced in the mid-1950s, when Al Pinaire, a police detective in Wichita, Kansas, saw it at a gun show there. Pinaire was a longtime gun collector who kept meticulous records of every weapon he bought, sold, or traded. After he died, his family found a large photo album containing scores of photographs of guns. Among them were photos of Hitler's pistol — one taken of each side of the gun. Included in the photographs, along the bottom, was a ruler that bore the words "WICHITA POLICE LABORATORY." Pinaire did not have the money to buy the pistol, but he persuaded the owner — whose identity was not recorded — to allow him to take it to the Wichita police station. Pinaire asked a crime-lab employee to photograph it because the lab had a better-quality camera.

There was no further news of the gun until February 1966, when the March issue of the men's magazine *Argosy* rolled off the presses, featuring a front page dominated by an oversized photograph of Hitler's pistol along with a black swastika and a picture of the Nazi leader.

The magazine said the pistol was going to be put up for sale by a Cleveland gun dealer. Buried on page 85 of the 144-page publication was an uncredited one-column article. The brevity of the article and its placement — given that the cover of the magazine was devoted to the story — suggested it was a last-minute, just-before-deadline addition to the issue.

The article was written in breathless prose.

"Surely the most successful souvenir hunter of World War II is the fellow, identity unknown, who copped Adolf Hitler's solid-gold 7.65-mm Walther automatic, shown on our cover, and brought it back to the States," it began.

The gun is the one that was presented to Hitler by the Walther Company on his fiftieth birthday — April 20, 1939 — and which he wore as his personal sidearm from then on. Hitler was a nut for uniforms, and having his solid-gold ivory-handled, monogrammed pistol strapped to his side must have added a little extra bounce to that famous strut of his.

It is possible that this weapon is the one with which he ended his life. The usual story of Hitler's death is that he shot himself in his bombproof bunker. Subsequently, the bunker was blown up, along with Hitler's body. The gold Walther is undamaged, however, though a laboratory check has revealed traces of human blood under the ivory hand grips.

Exactly who it was who "liberated" this weapon and brought it out of Germany is a question that is shrouded in mystery ... The present owners are Richard Elrad and Walter Woodford, who run an antique firearms and armor shop, The Musket and Lance, in Cleveland, Ohio. They acquired the gun from an undisclosed source, together

with several trunksful of miscellaneous items — silver-
ware, silver dishes, a tablecloth, some books, flags — all
of which has not been positively identified as Hitler's
personal property. The present owners refuse to disclose
how much they paid for the gun and the other items or to
speculate on what they might bring. They will only say
that the collection is "priceless."

In just the first two paragraphs, the article had made two
errors. The gun was not solid gold — it was gold-plated. And
Hitler did not carry the gun as his personal sidearm. But
those were minor mistakes compared to the egregious error
contained in the third paragraph. This was not the gun with
which Hitler committed suicide but rather the pistol that Teen
Palm had taken from Hitler's desk. Elrad and Woodford were
later quoted by newspaper reporters as saying they had purchased the trove of Hitler memorabilia two years earlier from
someone whose identity they declined to disclose.

In an attempt to confirm the gun's authenticity, Elrad traveled to London and to Munich, Hamburg, and Ulm in Germany. He showed photographs of the weapon to members of
the Walther family, who agreed it was the gun presented to
Hitler on his fiftieth birthday.

Elrad met with Heinz Linge, Hitler's personal valet, who
also confirmed the weapon was authentic. But he would not
say it was Hitler's suicide pistol.

Still, or perhaps to increase its value, Elrad insisted it was.

He and Woodford were selling the gun and other Nazi
booty, including a spade that Hitler was said to have used to
break ground for the Autobahn, a Nazi flag that storm troopers had presented to Hitler, and a statue of Ottilie "Tilly"
Fleischer, a famous German athlete who won a gold medal in

the javelin throw at Germany's 1936 Olympics. The statue, made by Joseph Thorak, one of the Nazi Party's official sculptors, was three feet high, and Fleischer was holding an Olympic wreath over her head.

Also up for sale were tablecloths made of white linen and damask — one of which had been presented to Hitler by Mussolini — as well as Hitler's personal silver, and a signed copy of *Mein Kampf.*

It was an amazing collection — so amazing that it seemed almost impossible that one person could have brought it all back from Germany by himself, as Elrad and Woodford insisted.

The *Argosy* article attracted considerable attention in the rare-gun collecting community, and particularly those who specialized in Nazi memorabilia. Among them was a Canadian named Andrew Wright, a gun and Nazi memorabilia collector from Swift Current, Saskatchewan. Wright was one of the largest collectors of Nazi memorabilia in North America. He kept it all on display in a museum on his farm outside of Swift Current. Spurred by the *Argosy* article, Wright and his wife drove to Cleveland.

After one look at the gun, Wright pronounced that he was ready to buy the entire collection if Elrad was ready to sell. After two hours of negotiation, they struck a bargain, and Wright paid $50,000 to buy the entire lot.

The gun was headed for Canada.

Wright considered the gun priceless. "This gun will put Swift Current on the map," he told a Swift Current newspaper. "There are hundreds of gun collectors in the United States who have never seen it and they will come up."

That dream of huge crowds of visitors never materialized, though, and in 1987, Wright decided to sell the gun. By that time, no one was claiming Hitler had committed suicide with it. A newspaper article reported that a person who wished to remain anonymous bought the gun for $114,000 — the highest price ever paid for an item of military memorabilia — and that the gun had been taken from Hitler's Munich apartment by American soldiers.

Since then, the gun has changed hands more than once. Australian construction magnate Warren Anderson owned it for a time. By 2010, the gun was in the hands of a collector who prefers to remain anonymous.

Richard Elrad, who journeyed to Germany to investigate the gun back in the 1960s, no longer lives in Cleveland. Years after the sale, he moved to a suburb of Atlanta. His partner in the sale is dead. Elrad still refuses to believe the gun Teen Palm brought back from Munich was the same weapon he sold to Andrew Wright in 1966. He insists that the gun he sold to Wright was not the weapon stolen from the Wood-bridge home. He asserts that he obtained the pistol from a U.S. Army colonel who kept it in a footlocker on his farm for two decades after the war. Elrad says he promised to keep the soldier's identity secret and he will not break that promise, even though he says the man is dead and has no living relatives. Elrad says he has a tape recording of an interview with the man in which the man says he found the gun in Hitler's office building, known as the Fuehrerbau. But he declines to share the tape.

Al Pinaire's photographs are fakes, Elrad says, even though at least two gun experts who have personally examined Hitler's pistol assert the photos are genuine. Elrad has a photocopy of a black-and-white photograph he says depicts an unidentified soldier holding Hitler's pistol. He says he looked at it with a magnifying glass, and it is the same gun he sold to Andrew Wright in 1966.

"History has a way of refashioning, burying, or confusing facts, especially when they concern something as potentially valuable as this gun," says John Woodbridge. "Initially, no person was going to say, 'I stole this gun from a house in Savannah.' And so other stories are spun. Perhaps one day the gun will resurface and the facts will become clear."

The principals in the story are all gone. Charles Woodbridge died in 1995 at the age of ninety-three; his wife, Ruth, died in 1962, shortly after she and her husband had visited the Palms in Germany. Helen Palm died in 1997, but her daughter, Susie, kept the voluminous correspondence between her parents and shared the letters with Woodbridge.

"These were revelatory," Woodbridge says. "Through them I was able to see the remarkable transformation of a talented but relatively aimless and self-doubting young man into a more confident person who could lead troops into mortal combat. This transformation was enhanced by his Christian conversion, his marriage to Helen, a great love story, and his actual experiences in warfare.

"Teen was a Christian who lived out his faith in an exemplary fashion. He wanted others to experience the same faith, but he never attempted to have this happen through any form of coercion or the exploitation of his rank as an officer. He was also a great American hero. My father had told one of my sisters that in the wake of the death of Captain Robertson, Teen volunteered for the dangerous, potentially suicidal mission to find and kill Hitler in Munich."

Woodbridge also gained a new appreciation for the sacrifice and bravery of the men and women who fought in World War II.

The last five years have also given him a deeper understanding of his own father.

"Yes, I learned things I never knew or understood before," he says. "This would include his ability to communicate with young men, and how deeply he participated in the life of the communities in which he ministered. I also came to a better sense of my father's personal Christian faith."

He talks about learning of what he calls the "good Germans," including those who risked their lives to try to destroy the Nazi infrastructure of Munich and who viewed the advancing American troops as liberators, not as foreign occupiers. And he says that inside the story of the "greatest manhunt in history" was the untold account that Hitler was once literally in the crosshairs of Rupprecht Gerngross's rifle.

He pauses for a moment and then says, "I have changed in the last five years, and I will undoubtedly continue to reflect upon Teen Palm's story of courage and faith for the rest of my life."

The voices on the television, talking of the usual contentiousness in the world, begin to fade as Woodbridge turns his attention to the snow falling gently outside the windows of his home. The winter scene evokes a word. That word is "peaceful," and it is a very good word.

AFTERWORD

TEEN PALM'S DAUGHTER, SUSIE, NOW LIVES IN NEW JERSEY
with her husband, Jonathan Wort, a New Jersey native with
a distinguished military career as a Navy and Marine Corps
pilot. They have three children, Joshua and Daniel, both of
whom are in the military, and Elizabeth, a college track and
cross-country coach.

As Palm's daughter, Susie grew up feeling very much a part
of the military family as well as part of the Christian community within that family. As a result, she fully expected and
hoped to marry into the military. When she turned twenty-
one, she felt rather disowned when her military-dependent
identification card expired.

And then, Jonathan came into her life.

They met on a blind date. Susie was working as a nurse
and Jonathan was a flight instructor for the U.S. Navy. His
military career had begun when he was commissioned as an
ensign in the United States Navy in 1970. He trained as a pilot
on the TA-4 Skyhawk and received his Naval Aviator wings
in 1972. After two years as an instructor, he joined Attack
Squadron 27 based at Naval Air Station Lemoore, California,
flying the A-7E Corsair II aircraft. The squadron, aboard the
USS *Enterprise*, embarked on the first peacetime cruise to the

Pacific, South China Sea, Coral Sea, and Indian Ocean following the Vietnam War and in 1976–77 participated in international fleet exercises with Australia, New Zealand, Singapore, and Iran.

Upon completion of that cruise, Jonathan, by then a lieutenant, transferred to the Naval Reserves and was assigned to Naval Air Station, Willow Grove, Pennsylvania. He and Susie wed in 1978, and in 1980 he transferred to the United States Marine Corps and was assigned to Marine Attack Squadron 131 flying the A-4E and A-4M Skyhawk.

Their first child, Joshua, was born in 1982, and their second, Elizabeth, was born the following year.

In 1987, promoted by then to lieutenant colonel, Jonathan assumed command of Marine Headquarters and Maintenance Squadron 42 in Willow Grove.

Jonathan's years of flying jets in the reserves surely influenced Joshua, who began expressing his desire to become a military pilot and attend a service academy when he was just a fourth grader. Susie often drove Joshua and Elizabeth to Willow Grove to watch Jonathan land after a flight.

On days when they did not make the trip, Susie and the children would dash to a window of their home after flashing the house flood lights to signal Jonathan as he flew overhead on his weekly training flights.

When he retired in 1989, Jonathan had more than thirty-five hundred flight hours, mostly in single-seat, single-engine jet aircraft, and he had made more than one hundred sixty carrier landings, fifty-eight of them at night.

That same year, their youngest child, Daniel, was born. Joshua was a major military influence in his younger brother's life. When Joshua was accepted at the United States Naval Academy in Annapolis, Maryland, the family visited frequently and attended Army-Navy football games in Philadelphia.

Elizabeth, a gifted runner, achieved much success in academics and athletics. She was a high school New Jersey state champion in several events as well as a high school All-American. She attended Duke University on an athletic scholarship and earned All-American status three times as well as competing in the 2008 Olympic Trials. She remains there as an assistant women's track and cross-country coach.

Both Joshua and Daniel were imbued with military spirit, even though neither Jonathan nor Susie intentionally pushed them toward military careers. Despite their strong ties to the military, Susie and Jonathan left the choice up to their boys.

Joshua was commissioned as a second lieutenant upon graduation from the Naval Academy in 2005. After attending the Basic Officer's Course in Quantico, Virginia, he reported to Naval Air Station, Pensacola, for flight training. Trained as a helicopter pilot, Joshua was designated a Naval Aviator in 2007. Now a captain in the Marine Corps, Joshua is assigned to Marine Heavy Helicopter Squadron 463. He has completed a seven-month deployment to Afghanistan in support of Operation Enduring Freedom, where he was designated a helicopter aircraft commander.

Daniel chose to follow in the military service footsteps of his grandfather, father, and older brother by entering the U.S. Marine Corps "Platoon Leader Class" program for officers. He completed two summers of Officer Candidate School at the Marine Corps Base Quantico, Virginia, and graduated in July 2010. Upon completion of his college education, he will be commissioned as a second lieutenant in the U. S. Marine Corps in 2011.

"As parents, you would never choose for your children to

expose themselves to the dangerous situations of a military career, but we totally support that choice as one of honor, courage, and opportunity to subdue evil and promote good," Susie says.

"More important to us than their career choices was the early decision of all three of our children, Joshua, Elizabeth, and Daniel, to accept Jesus Christ as their Savior and the Lord of their lives," she says. "That's the ultimate career choice. Their grandparents, Teen and Helen Palm, would find no greater joy than this."

Jonathan says, "A Bible verse that has been special to me all my life is Joshua 1:9 — 'Have I not commanded you? Be strong and of good courage; do not be afraid, nor be dismayed, for the Lord your God is with you wherever you go.' These young men have chosen to place their personal faith in Jesus Christ as their Lord and Savior and to be involved with the Officers' Christian Fellowship as they endeavor to serve God in the military. It is a privilege we share as father and sons to serve our country, but an even greater privilege to serve our God who created us, loves us, and has promised to be with us wherever we go."

As Helen Palm relied on her faith to sustain her when Teen went overseas to fight the Nazis, Susie does the same.

"I wasn't sure how I would handle Josh's first deployment to Afghanistan, but God proved Himself more than sufficient to calm my anxiety and to trust Him with the outcome," she said.

She saw his deployment as a new opportunity to grow in her faith, to encourage others to pray for him and his family, to support him with letters and care packages, and to visit his family in his absence.

The wintry days of early January 2011 found her reflecting on the future. "I am sure I will find the same source of strength as Josh deploys a second time and as Daniel is commissioned into the Marine Corps on his graduation from college," she said.

As she did when Joshua went to Afghanistan for his first tour, Susie turned to verses from Philippians 4:6–8, which reminded her not to worry, but instead to pray and to control her prone-to-wander thoughts:

> Be careful [anxious] for nothing; but in everything by prayer and supplication with thanksgiving let your requests be made known unto God. And the peace of God, which passeth all understanding, shall keep your hearts and minds through Christ Jesus. Finally, brethren, whatsoever things are true, whatsoever things are honest, whatsoever things are just, whatsoever things are pure, whatsoever things are lovely, whatsoever things are of good report; if there be any virtue, and if there be any praise, think on these things.

Susie is reminded of those "things" when she walks through her family room each day. On the wall hangs a case displaying her father's military medals.

For his courage, valor, and bravery.

They are a testament to his life, character, and legacy.

Teen Palm.

A courageous soldier of the Greatest Generation.

A true hero of the faith.

ACKNOWLEDGMENTS

WHAT A PERSONAL DELIGHT IT HAS BEEN TO PARTNER WITH Maurice Possley in crafting this book. Maurice is an incredible researcher and writer. In his capable hands, the story of Teen Palm came very much alive — birthed from letters, newspaper and magazine articles, journals and books and multiple interviews. My deepest thanks to Maurice for giving of his creative genius to the telling of this amazing story of faith and courage.

Thanks too to Maurice's friend Rick Kogan of the *Chicago Tribune* for his genuine insights concerning the writing of the manuscript.

I would like to express my deep gratitude to Susie Wort, Teen Palm's daughter, for her friendship, hospitality, and generosity in making available to Maurice and myself Teen Palm's papers — a veritable treasure trove of letters and photos.

Special thanks are in order to Moe Girkins, the President and CEO of Zondervan, for her personal support for this project from its inception and to Sue Brower, our skillful editor at Zondervan, for seeing the project to its completion.

A number of individuals were interviewed for this project. Some graciously made available their personal archives to us.

Dr. Jürgen Wittenstein was especially generous in sharing a portion of his life story.

Sincere thanks to my colleagues at Trinity, Scott Manetsch and Dennis Magary, and to my sisters, Pat, Rosemary, and Norma, who were all very supportive of this project. My sisters in particular provided invaluable firsthand knowledge about Teen Palm.

And finally, I would like to thank my wife, Susan, for her encouragement and wise counsel. I am grateful to God for her Christian example and her love. And so are her children.

JOHN WOODBRIDGE

THIS BOOK WOULD NOT HAVE COME TO LIFE WITHOUT THE aid, counsel, and reassurances of many people, but particularly Christopher Ferebee, my agent, for his integrity and perseverance; Cookie Ridolfi, my colleague, for her patience and understanding; Bob Richardson and Tatjana Vujosevic, my friends, for their generosity of spirit and use of their couch; and Rick Kogan for his wordsmithing genius and more importantly, a friendship that spans more than thirty years

I want to thank my extended family at Little Church by the Sea for prayers and support, particularly David and Lisa Burchi, David and Sarah Vanderveen, and Sarah Metherell.

The unexpected entry into my life of John Woodbridge, who came bearing this most extraordinary tale, is yet more proof that when we make plans, God laughs. I cannot thank John enough for his confidence in me.

I am indebted to Teen Palm's daughter, Susie, and her family for opening their hearts, sharing their memories, and entrusting me with the moving story of Teen Palm's courage and enduring faith.

I want to thank my son, Vasco Fitzmaurice Mark David Possley, who patiently and generously allowed me to spend hours at my desk working on this book. I love you very much.

In the mid-1990s, when I was a journalist in Chicago, I asked a young woman who was striving to become a religion writer how one would go about reconnecting with God.

"All you have to do is ask Him," she said.

She was right, I soon discovered.

For that moment alone, I will ever and utterly be thankful to my wife, Cathleen. For her support, counsel, patience, sharp eye for detail, and, most of all, her love, I am profoundly grateful.

MAURICE POSSLEY

SELECT BIBLIOGRAPHY

Ambrose, Stephen E. *Band of Brothers* (New York: Simon & Schuster, 2001).

Ambrose, Stephen E. *D-Day, June 6, 1944: The Climactic Battle of World War II* (New York: Simon & Schuster, 1994).

Baigent, Michael, and Leigh, Richard. *Secret Germany: Stauffenberg and the True Story of Operation Valkyrie* (New York: Skyhorse, 2008).

Barnhart, Lt. Robert M. *Personal History of the 179th Regiment, Company B.* http//www.45thdivision.org/Veterans/Barnhart179.htm

Beevor, Antony. *D-Day: The Battle for Normandy* (New York: Viking Penguin, 2009).

Biddiscome, Perry. *The Last Nazis: SS Werewolf Guerrilla Resistance in Europe 1944–1947* (Stroud, Gloucestershire: Tempus, 2004).

Bishop, Leo V., Fisher, George A., Glasgow, Frank J. *The Fighting Forty-Fifth: The Combat Report of an Infantry Division* (Baton Rouge, La.: Army & Navy Publishing Company, 1946).

Bon, Keith E. *When the Odds Were Even: The Vosges Mountains Campaign (October 1944 – January 1945)* (New York: Ballantine, 2006).

Breitman, Richard, et al. *U.S. Intelligence and the Nazis* (Cambridge: Cambridge University Press, 2005).

Buechner, Emajean. *Sparks: The Combat Diary of a Battalion Commander (Rifle), WWII, 157ᵗʰ Infantry Regiment, 45ᵗʰ Division, 1941 – 1945* (Metairie, La.: Thunderbird, 1993).

Burleigh, Michael and Wippermann, Wolfgang. *The Racial State Germany 1933 – 1945* (Cambridge: Cambridge University Press, 2007).

Calhoun, Dr. David B. *Splendor of Grace*: *Independent Presbyterian Church 1755 – 2005* (Greenville, S.C.: A Press Printing, 2005).

Dann, Sam, ed. *Dachau, 29 April 1945: The Rainbow Liberation Memoirs* (Lubbock, Tex.: Texas Tech University Press, 1998).

Dietrich, Otto. *Hitler* (Chicago: Regnery, 1955).

Dumbach, Annette and Newborn, Jud. *Sophie Scholl and the White Rose* (Oxford: Oneworld, 2006).

Ellis, John. *The Sharp End: The Fighting Man in World War II* (London: Aurum, 2009).

Evans, Richard J. *The Coming of the Third Reich* (New York: Penguin, 2004).

Evans, Richard J. *The Third Reich at War* (New York: Penguin, 2009).

Evans, Richard J. *The Third Reich in Power, 1933 – 1939* (New York: Penguin, 2005).

Fest, Joachim. *Hitler*. Trans., Richard and Clara Winston (San Diego: Harcourt, 1974).

Fest Joachim. *Plotting Hitler's Death: The Story of the German Resistance*. Trans. Bruce Little (New York: Holt, 1996).

The First Presbyterian Church of Flushing, N.Y. *Seventy-Fifth Anniversary 1905–1980* (Hackensack, N.J.: Custombook, Inc., 1980).

Fritz, Stephen G. *Endkampf Soldiers, Civilians and the Death of the Third Reich* (Lexington, Ky.: University Press of Kentucky, 2004).

Gerngross, Rupprecht. *Aufstand der Freiheits Aktion Bayern 1945: "Fasanenjagd" und wie die Münchner Freiheit ihren Namen bekam* (Augsburg, Germany: Heidrich, 1995).

Gisevius, Hans Bernd. *Valkryrie: An Insider's Account of the Plot to Kill Hitler.* Trans., Richard and Clara Winston (Philadelphia: Da Capo, 2009).

Goodrick-Clarke, Nicholas. *The Occult Roots of Nazism: Secret Aryan Cults and Their Influence on Nazi Ideology* (Washington Square, N.Y.: New York University Press, 1992).

Hamann, Brigitte. *Winfred Wagner: A Life at the Heart of Hitler's Bayreuth.* Trans., Alan Bance (Orlando: Harcourt, 2005).

Hamerow, Theodore. *On the Road to the Wolf's Lair: German Resistance to Hitler* (Cambridge, Mass.: Belknap Press of Harvard University Press, 1999).

Hastings, Max. *Armageddon: The Battle for Germany, 1944–1945* (New York: Knopf, 2004).

Hayes, Peter and Roth, John, eds.. *The Oxford Handbook of Holocaust Studies* (New York: Oxford University Press, 2010).

Hayman, Ronald. *Hitler + Geli* (New York: Bloomsbury, 1997).

Heideking, Jürgen and Mauch, Christof, eds. *American Intelligence and the German Resistance to Hitler* (Boulder, Co.: Westview, 1998).

Heidenberger, Felix. *Mau Yee Münchner Freiheit* (Berlin: Pro Business GmbH, 2004).

Heidenberger, Peter. *From Munich to Washington: A German American Memoir* (np: XLIBRIS, 2004).

Hell's Angels — 303rd Bomb Group. http://www.303rdbg.com.

Hesketh, Roger. *Fortitude: The D-Day Deception Campaign* (Woodstock, Vt.: Overlook, 2002).

Hinsley, F. H. *British Intelligence in the Second World War* (London: HMSO, 1994).

Hirshson, Stanley P. *General Patton: A Soldier's Life* (New York: HarperCollins, 2002).

History of the 45th Infantry Division. http://www.45thdivision.org/history.htm.

The History Place (Nazi Germany/World War II, http://www.history place.com).

"Hitler's Golden Gun," *Argosy* (March 1966): 85.

Hoffmann, Peter. *Hitler's Personal Security: Protecting the Führer, 1921 – 1945* (Cambridge, Mass.: MIT Press, 1979).

Hynes, Samuel (Introduction). *Reporting World War II: American Journalism 1938 – 1946* (New York: Literary Classics of America, 2001).

"Invasion," *Life* (June 12, 1944): 27 – 46.

Israel, David I. *The Day the Thunderbird Cried: Untold Stories of World War II* (np: Emek, 2005).

Kershaw, Ian. *Hitler.* 2 vols. (New York: Norton, 2000).

Kershaw, Ian. *Popular Opinion and Political Dissent in Third Reich* (Oxford: Clarendon Press, 2002).

Kopleck, Mark. *Past Finder: Munich 1933 – 1945* (Berlin: Ch. Links Verlag, nd).

Korner-Kalman, Anneliese. *Across the Street from Adolf Hitler: A Memoir* (np: XLIBRIS, 2001).

"Landings in Normandy," *Life* (June 19, 1944): 25–38.

Large, David Clay. *Where Ghosts Walked: Munich's Road to the Third Reich* (New York: Norton, 1997).

Linge, Heinz. *With Hitler to the End: The Memoirs of Adolf Hitler's Valet*. Trans. Geoffrey Brooks (London: Frontline, 2009).

Linn, Jo White. *First Presbyterian Church Salisbury, North Carolina, and Its People 1821–1995* (Salisbury, N.C.: privately published, 1996).

Lutzer, Erwin W. *Hitler's Cross* (Chicago: Moody, 1995).

Mauch, Christof. *The Shadow War against Hitler: The Covert Operations of America's Wartime Secret Intelligence Service*. Trans., Jeremiah M. Riemer (New York: Columbia University Press, 2003).

McNamara, Bernard. Unpublished correspondence and personal diary.

Metaxas, Eric. *Bonhoeffer: Pastor, Martyr, Prophet, Spy* (Nashville: Nelson, 2010).

Mitchell, Arthur H. *Hitler's Mountain: The Führer, Obersalzberg and the American Occupation of Berchtesgaden* (Jefferson, N.C.: McFarland, 2007).

Moorhouse, Roger. *Killing Hitler: The Plots, the Assassins, and the Dictator Who Cheated Death* (New York: Bantam, 2007).

Munsell, Warren P., Jr. *The Story of a Regiment: A History of the 179th Regimental Combat Team* (New York: Warren P. Munsell Jr., 1946).

Nelson, Guy. *Thunderbird: A History of the 45th Infantry Division* (Oklahoma City: Colographics, 1970).

Novotny, Patrick. *This Georgia Rising: Education, Civil Rights, and the Politics of Change in Georgia in the 1940s* (Macon, Ga.: Mercer University Press, 2007).

"Our World-Wide War," *Life* (June 26, 1944): 21 – 33, 43 – 46.

Overseas Press Club of America. *Deadline Delayed* (New York: Dutton, 1947).

Overy, R. J. *The Origins of the Second World War*. 2nd edition (London: Longman, 1998).

Palm, Ira. Unpublished letters and papers.

Penrose, Antony, ed. *Lee Miller's War: Photographer and Correspondent with the Allies in Europe 1944 – 1945* (London: Thames & Hudson, 2008).

Perry, Mark. *Partners in Command: George Marshall and Dwight Eisenhower in War and Peace* (New York: The Penguin Press, 2007).

Perry, Michael, ed.. *Dachau Liberated: The Official Report by the U.S. Seventh Army* (Seattle: Inkling, 2000).

Petersen, Neal H., ed. *From Hitler's Doorstep: The Wartime Intelligence Reports of Allen Dulles, 1942 – 1945* (University Park, Pa.: The Pennsylvania State University Press, 1996).

Petrova, Ada and Watson, Peter. *The Death of Hitler: The Full Story with New Evidence from Secret Russian Archives* (New York: Norton, 1995).

Pope, Ernest R. *Munich Playground* (New York: Putnam, 1941).

Quinn, William W. *"Buffalo Bill": Buffalo Bill Remembers Truth and Courage* (Fowlerville, Mich.: Wilderness Adventure, 1991).

Rankin, James L. *Walther, Volume II: Engraved, Presentation and Standard Models* (Coral Gables, Fla.: np, nd).

Ravenscroft, Trevor. *The Spear of Destiny* (Boston, Weiser, 1973).

Rawson, Andrew. *In Pursuit of Hitler: A Battle Field Guide to Bavaria* (Barnsley, South Yorkshire: Pen & Sword Military, 2008).

Report of Operations: The Seventh United States Army in France and Germany 1944–1945, Vol. II (Nashville: Battery, 1988).

Robbins, Christopher. *Test of Courage: The Michel Thomas Story* (New York: Free Press, 2000).

Rosenfeld, Gavriel D. *Munich and Memory: Architecture, Monuments, and the Legacy of the Third Reich* (Berkeley: University of California Press, 2000).

Rush, Robert S. *The U.S. Infantryman in World War II* (Oxford, Osprey, 2003).

Sayer, Ian and Botting, Douglas. *America's Secret Army: The Untold Story of the Counter Intelligence Corps* (New York: Franklin Watts, 1989).

Sayre, Joel, "Letter from Munich," *The New Yorker* (May 19, 1945): 61.

Scholl, Inge. *The White Rose: Munich 1942–1943.* Trans., Arthur R. Schultz (Middletown, Conn.: Wesleyan University Press, 1983).

Schroeder, Christa. *He Was My Chief: The Memoirs of Adolf Hitler's Secretary* (London: Frontline, 2009).

Shirer, William L. *The Rise and Fall of the Third Reich* (New York: Simon & Schuster, 1990).

Spoede, Dr. Robert W. *More than Conquerors: A History of Officers' Christian Fellowship of the U.S.A. With a Special Report by the OCF Editors on the Years 1984–1993* (Englewood, Colo.: OCF, 1993).

Stafford, David. *Endgame, 1945* (New York: Little, Brown, 2007).

Stars and Stripes. The Story of the 45th Infantry Division (Whitefish, Mont.: Kessinger, nd).

Tuck, Stephen G. N. *Beyond Atlanta: The Struggle for Racial Equality in Georgia, 1940–1980* (Athens, Ga.: The University of Georgia Press, 2003).

Tyson, Joseph Howard. *Hitler's Mentor: Dietrich Eckart, His Life, Times & Milieu* (New York: iUniverse, 2008).

Von Klemperer, Klemens. *German Resistance against Hitler: The Search for Allies Abroad, 1938–1945* (Oxford: Clarendon Press, 1992).

"The War Ends in Europe," *Life* magazine (May 14, 1945): 27–98.

Weintraub, Stanley. *Eleven Days in December: Christmas at the Bulge, 1944* (New York: Caliber, 2006).

Whiting, Charles. *America's Forgotten Army: The Story of the U.S. Seventh* (New York: Sarpedon, 1999).

Whitlock, Flint. *The Rock of Anzio from Sicily to Dachau: A History of the U.S. 45th Infantry Division* (Boulder, Colo.: Westview, 1998).

Wilson, James. *Hitler's Alpine Retreat* (Havertown, Pa.: Casemate, 2005).

Woodbridge, Charles. Unpublished letters, sermons, and diary.

Written accounts from Norma Woodbridge, Pat Woodbridge Hearle, and Rosemary Woodbridge.

Newspapers as sourced by NewspaperARCHIVE.com

Share Your Thoughts

With the Author: Your comments will be forwarded to the author when you send them to *zauthor@zondervan.com*.

With Zondervan: Submit your review of this book by writing to *zreview@zondervan.com*.

Free Online Resources at
www.zondervan.com

Zondervan AuthorTracker: Be notified whenever your favorite authors publish new books, go on tour, or post an update about what's happening in their lives at www.zondervan.com/authortracker.

Daily Bible Verses and Devotions: Enrich your life with daily Bible verses or devotions that help you start every morning focused on God. Visit www.zondervan.com/newsletters.

Free Email Publications: Sign up for newsletters on Christian living, academic resources, church ministry, fiction, children's resources, and more. Visit www.zondervan.com/newsletters.

Zondervan Bible Search: Find and compare Bible passages in a variety of translations at www.zondervanbiblesearch.com.

Other Benefits: Register yourself to receive online benefits like coupons and special offers, or to participate in research.

ZONDERVAN®

ZONDERVAN.com/
AUTHORTRACKER
follow your favorite authors